The Brand Called You

Personal Marketing for Financial Advisors

Peter Montoya & Tim Vandehey

MILLENNIUM ADVERTISING

The Financial Services Advertising Agency

www.milladv.com

Books are available for bulk purchases at special discounts. For information, please contact Millennium Advertising at 888-730-5300 or info@milladv.com.

FIRST EDITION PUBLISHED 1999
8 6 4 2 0 9 7 5 3 1
ISBN 0-9674506-0-8
Library of Congress Catalog Card Number: 99-90875
Printed in the United States of America

This publication is designed to provide accurate and authoritative information with regard to the subject matter covered. It is sold with the understanding that the publisher is not engaged in rendering legal, accounting or other professional advice. If legal advice or other exert assistance is required, the services of a competent professional person should be sought.

—From a Declaration of Principles jointly adopted by a Committee of the American Bar Association and a Committee of Publishers and Associations

Book Designed by Andrew Rea & Shelly Beck
Edited by Anthony Ross

www.thebrandcalledyou.com

Advance Praise for The Brand Called You

"Any financial professional who doesn't read the book is asking to be overtaken by smart marketers who are capable of eating his lunch and leaving him in the dust."

Richard Pascuzzi
Addison Securities
Director of Marketing

"Personal Marketing is rocket fuel for the businesses of financial planners who have the vision and determination to put it into practice."

Chris Ranney
Brecek & Young Advisors
Executive Vice President

"Make more money, spend less time doing it. It's very possible with Personal Marketing, which shows you how to make prospects come to you, instead of you chasing them."

Norlyn Feldman
Cadaret, Grant & Co.
Senior Vice President

"Dull, boilerplate marketing has become an endangered species with the publication of 'The Brand Called You.'"

Nancy J. Johnson, CFP
Cambridge Investment Research, Inc.
Vice President, Director of Compliance

"No previous book I've read is better or more honest about the need for advisors to think of themselves as small businesses. This book is a must-read for any rep planning to stay in business."

Gordon Dunne
Financial Services Network
Senior Vice President, Managing Director

"Finally, a book that understands that people, not products, are the heart of all effective marketing! These ideas and methods are going to change financial services."

Joby Gruber
Financial Services Corporation
Senior Vice President & Chief Marketing Officer

"Nothing I've ever read is better at telling advisors the hard truth about their changing industry, and giving them critical survival tips."

Daniel Flynn
First Montauk Securities
Vice President Financial Services

"An extraordinary collection of out-of-the-box marketing thinking that promises to turn careers around and make some advisors rich..."

Chris Davis
ICIMC
Executive Director

"The process of attracting and retaining clients can be most effectively through Personal Marketing..."

Richard H. Ford
IRM Distributors, Inc.
Senior Vice President, Sales & Marketing

"No technique cuts through the noise and clutter of today's advertising jumble like Personal Marketing. It's an incredible way for reps to get noticed."

Dana L. Woodbury
Multi-Financial Securities Corp.
Senior Vice President of Equity Sales

"Inside tips on writing, printing, mailing and prospecting in one easy-to-read, advisor friendly package…"

Jay Lewis
Nathan & Lewis Securities
Chairman & President

"By reading this book and understanding positioning, financial advisors will discover how to create brand images that clients find irresistible."

Shawn Dreffein, JD, CPA, CLU
National Planning Corporation
Senior Vice President, Marketing

"Less expensive than a Marketing course and a whole lot more practical, this little book contains a wealth of information including tips on writing, printing, mailing and prospecting in one easy-to-read, advisor-friendly package…"

Andrea Ruesch
New England Securities
Vice President

"Marketing is the focal point of building your business and this book makes you think about marketing in new ways."

Jon Buss
Offerman & Company
Senior Vice President

"The Brand Called You is the ultimate reference tool for any financial advisor wishing to develop an effective marketing game plan."

Erinn J. Ford
Pacific West Securities, Inc.
Vice President of Marketing

"Wise, sarcastic, glib, entertaining, no nonsense. An amazing collection of out-of-the-box marketing thinking. A must read."

James H. Dresselaers
Polaris Financial Services, Inc.
President

"Too much money has been spent by top producers to market themselves in ineffective ways. A guidebook like "A Brand Called You" is long overdue as it teaches financial professionals how to market better while saving money."

Robert W. Canfield, Jr.
Signator Financial Network
General Director

"If you want to be on the cutting edge of financial services marketing there is only one thing you need do: read "The Brand Called You.""

Fred Curly Morrison
Transamerica Financial Resources
Vice President, National Sales Director

Contents

The Brand Called You

Forward

In today's financial services world, the role of the full-service investment advisor is changing dramatically. Online trading firms offer transactions seemingly free of charge. Discount brokers and no-load mutual funds are offering more and more self-help services – and are even coming close to offering personal advice. Gone are the days when an advisor or broker could expect to make a decent living helping an investor complete a transaction. There are too many low-priced competitors who will do that, and more. Gone, too, are the days when the reputation of a brokerage firm's name was enough for brokers to attract clients. Wall Street's history of scandalous industry-wide behavior hasn't helped the industry's image. And upstart competitors, from investment advisory firms and independent brokers, to banks and accounting firms, offer the investing public alternative reputable financial service providers.

The commodization of transactions and products, and the growing choices available to consumers, has made personal branding more important than ever. Personal branding isn't anything new– it's how you as a broker or advisor have always related to individual clients. They see you as a person. Your personal attributes and how you communicate with clients is the reason they do business with you. Good investment advisors have always known this.

But how do you market "The Brand Called You"? That's what this book is about. Peter Montoya and Tim Vandehey show how to sell yourself to potential investment clients who don't yet know you personally. It's a different approach from the usual product marketing and firm advertising. But it's the right approach. Because customers aren't buying products and they're not buying a firm--they're buying you.

Dan Jamieson
Registered Representative Magazine
Editor in Chief

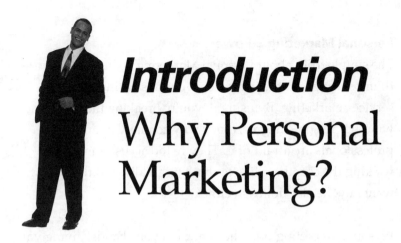

Introduction
Why Personal Marketing?

Say Good-bye to What You Know

Maybe your broker-dealer or your colleagues have given you a lot of marketing advice. Maybe you've been given none and been forced to learn on your own. Or maybe marketing has barely entered your mind until now. Well, you just made the best move possible for your career by opening this book. We're going to show you how to wipe your mind clean of conflicting or ineffective marketing advice, and we're going to show you what works for financial professionals. It's called Personal Marketing.

This book isn't about questioning what you've done in the past. It's about exploding some marketing myths, giving you new insights into how consumers react to you, and showing you that you are your own best product. It's about learning a new way to promote yourself, and grow your business like you've never dreamed possible.

Personal Marketing = Power

The simple truth about Personal Marketing is that it deliberately thumbs its nose at the typical conventions of financial services marketing. By using it, you're breaking the rules, and winning. To some degree, that's why so many financial professionals are afraid of it. They're too accustomed to walking the corporate line to think originally, and they don't want anyone else doing so either.

Personal Marketing puts the control in your hands, giving you the power to create your image, mold the way people think of you, and be as bold or conservative as you like. The point is, you're making the decisions, and you are the focus of your marketing efforts. Not products, not promises of fat returns, and not your corporate parent or brokerage. Personal Marketing is all about you.

Nothing Happens Until a Product is...Marketed?

Through thousands of hours of sales training we've been taught that, "nothing ever happens until a product or service is sold." Incorrect. These days, people are rarely "sold" on anything. Do you remember the last time you walked into a clothing store and a salesperson said "Hello"? You mumbled, "Just looking" and walked away. Why? Because thanks to being bombarded with advertising and direct marketing 24/7, Americans have the highest sales resistance in the world. Selling to us is rough, which is why the road warrior with his sample case is going the way of the dinosaur.

So why do Americans still spend discretionary income at a record-breaking pace? Because of marketing. Instead of being sold directly, we are exposed repeatedly to marketing messages that do two things: create a psychological need or urgency in us, and touch our emotions in some way. After enough exposure, some of us make a conscious decision, perhaps do some research, and then buy the product or service. In this day and age, people sell themselves.

Financial services is no different. Your marketing must pre-sell you—not your company—to a client over time. Done properly, Personal Marketing gets prospects to like and trust you before they've ever met you, allowing you to close them in person with some mild selling and confidence building. Wouldn't you love to have prospects 90% closed before they come through your door?

Market or Die

In today's fiercely competitive financial services environment, marketing is no longer an optional activity. It's a matter of survival. The consolidation of the industry by global insurance companies, and the rise of new sources of information such as powerful investment Web sites, means you're at risk of being turned into a commodity like pork bellies or petroleum. When that happens, you lose, because the financial firms with the biggest marketing dollars or the best-known brands will get all the best clients. You'll be left with the dregs and the bottom-feeders. You must begin marketing effectively today in a way that sets you apart, or chances are you'll be forced out of business.

You've heard the "ABC" Principle: Always Be Closing. We have a new one: "ABM," or Always Be Marketing. You should be marketing every day, whether that means networking at a local business luncheon or sending out a new direct mailer. If you plan on being in this business, you must commit 20-35% of your time, money and resources to marketing. If you are not marketing everyday, you are on a direct road to failure.

Everyone Wants Your Turf

United States financial advisors are among the highest paid professionals in the world. You're in one of the most lucrative, sought-after, and prestigious careers, and everyone wants what you have. There are thousands of people looking to take money out of your pocket and put you out of business. Some of your competition:

1. Wirehouse Stockbrokers: They are receiving the training, software, products and services they need to become more planning and relationship oriented.

2. Online Trading Sites: Not just for Web fanatics any more, these companies are gaining prestige and market share every day.

3. Banks & Credit Unions: These companies have a long list of existing clients, good reputations, distribution systems and deep pockets, enabling them to steal your clients.

4. CPAs: They have a three-year degree, trusting relationships with their clients, and are looking to expand their income beyond tax season.

5. Insurance Agents: Tired of being limited to proprietary insurance products, they are expanding their product and service lines quickly.

6. Financial Planners: Long the last word in financial services, your direct competitors are now losing ground to increasingly sophisticated competition.

The lesson? Having a client today doesn't mean that you'll have that client tomorrow. In addition to targeting prospects and getting new clients, you need to maintain your presence with your current clients, to educate them on the value that you provide. The above competitors are eyeing your clients right now as prime targets, and you can either secure your clients using strong, consistent marketing or lose them to someone else.

Marketing is Hard to Do...Or Is It?

You must market yourself. It's almost a law of nature. You must do it consistently, and you must do it before the competition comes calling and makes you too busy struggling to survive to worry about fancy logos and clever direct mail programs. However, we understand that you might be reluctant. Marketing seems hard for financial advisors, because you leave the safe realm of being a trusted advisor and enter the shady territory of sales. When you're a trusted financial ally, clients return your calls. Prospects don't. Clients listen to what you say because they are paying for it; prospects often think it's a come-on. To a client you are an authority, to a prospect you just look like another salesman out to make a score. The potential for rejection, and the idea that marketing is something arcane and sophisticated that should be left to huge ad agencies, is what scares many financial professionals away from marketing. But with Personal Marketing, you don't come across as a salivating salesman out to add to his quota. You come across as a person, a real human being who has things in common with his prospects. There's less chance of rejection, because Personal Marketing is designed to engender trust. As for creativity, you still need it. But as we walk you through each step of Personal Marketing, you'll come to understand that you don't have to be an advertising executive with twenty years in the business to develop a strong marketing campaign.

Practice Makes Perfect

Marketing offers no guarantees. Neither do we. You can receive the best advice in the world, but you've still got to go out and execute well and consistently. We will promise this: the more you market, the better you'll get. Even the best baseball players strike out, but you can't get a hit unless you come to bat. It's the same in marketing. You'll still strike out, but this book will help you increase your batting average. And just like in baseball, the more you practice (and research, and learn), the better you'll get.

Keep this in mind as well: marketing is hard work. There are no magic bullets. When a financial advisor hits a grand slam it is the result of diligent planning and hard work. Unlike sales where one unit of effort yields one unit of results, marketing gives you multiple units of results, but only after substantial amounts of time and resources have been invested.

Now's the Time to Take a Different Direction

Personal Marketing demands that you start thinking in new ways, and by starting this book, that's precisely what you're doing. When you finish this book, you'll be thinking like a marketer, not just a financial professional. You'll think in terms not just of securities and ROI, but in terms of target audiences and brand equity.

If you have not begun to market yourself, now is the time to start. Every day you delay is a missed opportunity. Use your competitors' complacency to your advantage, because they're not going to sleep forever.

How We Developed This Information

There's nothing like hands-on experience. As an advertising agency specializing in financial services, we face the same marketing challenges you face, and develop solutions for them. We have learned much of our financial services marketing by doing, but behind it all is a solid base of classical marketing training. We read books, attend workshops, and stay current with the top trade publications. With our blend of training and hands-on experience we have developed both the principles and the methods for financial advisors to dramatically change how they do business.

All right, let's get in to the principles, the practice, and the tools of Personal Marketing. Say goodbye to the way you used to think about your financial practice. You'll never look at it the same way again.

Peter Montoya
Tim Vandehey
September 1999

Part I
Personal Marketing Basics

CHAPTER ONE

Personal Marketing 101
You Are The Product

Ever hear of "Death of a Salesman"? It's a classic American play, but it could also be the title of the story of the typical financial advisor. You see, most advisors—probably including you—take the sales approach to building their business and finding new clients. That means cold calling, sending out the occasional Sales Letter, and a lot of door knocking and legwork. It means chasing after clients like a hound on a scent. It's time consuming and not very effective. And in a financial industry where competition grows by the day, the sales approach is a waste of your time and money. It's also a one-way ticket to the death of your business.

We're here to talk about marketing. Personal Marketing, to be exact. Where sales "chases" prospects, Personal Marketing "attracts" them. It's a unique approach that uses your personal background and personality – instead of dry facts about financial products and your broker-dealer – to make a one-to-one connection with your prospect and break through his natural sales resistance. Personal Marketing uses human-scale story telling, careful selection of the audience for your marketing, and disciplined, consistent execution to bring prospects to your door, 90% closed and ready to become clients. Sales can't and will never do that.

Glossary

Personal Marketing: Using your personal traits to create a unique brand identity in the minds of your target audience. Personal Marketing applies to all personal professional service providers including: medical professionals, lawyers, realtors, consultants & contractors.

Personal Marketing is About You

Conventional marketing for financial professionals means boring boilerplate brochures that talk products and make no personal connection whatsoever with the consumer. Personal Marketing does the opposite, making you the product and using your background, upbringing, education, hobbies, lifestyle, and experiences to make a personal connection with the reader, and to make him think, "This is someone I would like to work with."

Two fundamental principles about Personal Marketing you must know and absorb:
- You are your best and only product.
- People only work with people they like.

Personal Marketing uses your unique personal story to create an equally unique "personal brand" for you, an image that prospects immediately recognize as exclusive to you, and one that gets a strong, positive emotional and intellectual reaction. You're working with people, so you must sell to people first, not their investments. That's what Personal Marketing is all about.

Creating Your "Personal Brand"

Throughout this book, you'll see us discuss your "brand." We're not talking about toothpaste or detergent. Any product – including a financial advisor – has a brand identity, a set of characteristics that consumers use to identify with that product. For example, in the financial world Charles Schwab has a brand identity that's associated with customer-friendliness, low cost, and trust. That brand didn't come about by accident, but was carefully built through a blend of savvy marketing, public relations, and his company backing up its talk with good performance.

In this book, you'll learn how to create your own personal brand. Doing it takes a candid, honest examination of how prospects and clients perceive you today, and how you want them to perceive you in the future. Once you've determined the brand identity that's right for you, you must cultivate the characteristics you want the public to identify with you – expertise with technology, family man, multiple language speaker, tax expert, or whatever works for your overall marketing strategy. The stronger your brand identity, the more likely people are to think of you when they think of financial services. Owning that kind of "mind share" is one of the keys to long-term success and growth.

Your Image: Your Real Product

Earlier, we stated that you were your most important product. Actually, your image is your product, because that's how people perceive you. Think about it: your knowledge of financial services or your access to products doesn't give you a strategic advantage. Nearly every financial advisor in the country has the same access to products, services and information. And these days, so do the consumers.

People are going to choose to work with you based on your personal image. From there, you can use your knowledge of products and your commitment to service to keep them happy. But until you've got them signed as clients, consider everything you do part of your personal image:

1. Grooming
2. Clothes
3. Car
4. House
5. Verbal and written communication skills
6. Education
7. Your office
8. The professionalism of your staff

Any one of these, left to chance, can break you. Pay attention to them all as parts of your personal image. And if you doubt that people will decide whether or not to work with you based on how you speak on the phone, trust us. They already have.

People Do Business With People They Like

Think about the service providers you choose. Your mechanic. Your physician. Your real estate agent. No matter how skilled they were, would you work with them if they made you feel stupid, unimportant, or angry? Of course not. Financial services work the same way. It's a business built on relationships, and people only form relationships with people they like.

That's a fact that's quickly forgotten in the battle for clients. Advisors quickly retreat to what they know: selling products, selling services, or selling the company that backs them. Meanwhile, the advisors who are getting the best clients are doing what you should be doing: creating marketing that builds familiarity, commonality, and trust – the foundations for long-term relationships where both parties enjoy working together.

Trust: The Key to Advice

Author and speaker Nick Murray explains it best. A financial advisor's most important service is advice. When clients trust us, they're more likely to accept our advice, allowing us to provide them with something of value. When our clients trust us, we can guide them to use the right products, services and information to their benefit.

There are two stages to building this kind of trust:

1. Using Personal Marketing to create an image that tells the consumer that you're a good guy, and that they can trust you not to waste their time if they come into your office to listen to what you have to say.

2. Using your personal charm, your sales skills and your knowledge to provide consistently solid advice and results leading to long-term trust that you can perform as advertised.

In a world of ferocious competition for investor "mind share," your best (and only) product is yourself. Use it. Through Personal Marketing, you can create the foundation for the kind of strong, long term client relationships that will ensure you a thriving practice no matter what direction markets may take.

Applied Personal Marketing

In the practical sense, Personal Marketing means creating marketing materials such as brochures, direct mail cards and logos that use your personal story, rather than product or corporate information, as their contents. Using your lifestyle, background, and so on, you create a human, accessible, "Hey, this guy is just like me" image for yourself in all your materials. In any good Personal Marketing piece, the content is 90% personal, 10% sales pitch.

The other major part of Personal Marketing deals with deploying your materials. You'll develop a strategic mailing plan, choose target groups of prospects, and distribute your marketing materials according to a set schedule. Personal Marketing depends on two fundamental ideas: personalization and consistency. Tell your personal story, and then spread the word consistently. Without both, it's ineffective.

Personal Marketing Makes "Un" Common Sense

Personal Marketing seems utterly against the marketing common sense that's been ingrained into most financial professionals. You've been taught that people want to know about your product, your experience, your firm, the types of service you offer, and so on. And to some degree, that's true. But those are details for a face-to-face meeting with the prospect when you can temper these boring details—and get around people's natural sales resistance—with your personality and your practiced sales approach.

Glossary

Mindshare: A marketing term which refers to the prominence of a product's position in its audience's mind, or simply, how often a group of people thinks of a certain product or company when the entire category is mentioned. For example, Coca-Cola has tremendous mind share among cola drinkers, while RC Cola has poor mind share. Your goal is to get the largest mind share possible among your audience.

Marketing Versus Sales: Marketing Comes First

Marketing is the art and science of systematically attracting clients, like a magnet attracts iron filings. Sales is the activity of chasing down clients like hounds chasing down a hare during a hunt. Which takes more effort and offers greater rewards? Look at it this way: can the hounds chase down more than one hare at a time? No, but you can market to thousands simultaneously.

Marketing is about "owning" a piece of your prospect's mind, as well as your current client's mind, since you'll want to market to your current clients to keep them in the fold and to get referrals. In shorthand, that means that your clients and prospects think of your name as synonymous with financial services, at least for them in their personal world. It's similar in principle to some consumer products that have gone from brand names to generic terms: Xerox, Kleenex, Q-Tips. These are all brands that have become so familiar that we now ask someone to "Xerox this for me." In your Personal Marketing, over time, owning a piece of your client's mind should be your goal.

Visibility is More Important than Ability

It's a fact that galls people, but it's true. Being the best doesn't guarantee success. You could be the greatest financial advisor in the world and go broke. The most successful people in any business aren't always the most talented – in fact, they're rarely the most talented. Instead, success usually translates into being known, being perceived as something or someone that people must have, or creating a sense of urgency in the mind of the consumer. Look at Madonna or Arnold Schwarzenegger. Exceptionally talented artists? Of course not. Brilliant at self-promotion and awareness building? Definitely. McDonald's is another perfect example. No one with functioning taste buds would suggest that their burgers are the best, but they sell millions of them around the world every day. Why? Marketing. They've created a family-friendly brand identity which people identify almost exclusively with the Golden Arches. It's brilliant marketing.

Financial services are no different. To succeed, you must be known. You must be perceived by your prospects as a unique individual, a "caring person" who just happens also to be a whiz when it comes to selecting mutual funds or planning retirement accounts. Of course, once you've attracted the clients with your message, you must be a capable financial advisor to keep them. But getting your message out consistently and powerfully is where it all begins.

Case Study: Tom Gau

If you're going to hold up anyone as a model for the success of marketing for financial advisors, you'd be hard-pressed to find a better example than Tom Gau. The guru of the "million dollar boot camp," where he passes on his wisdom to success-minded financial advisors, has raked in a cool $3 million in gross dealer concessions in 1998 and 1999, while meeting with clients only four days out of every two weeks. In a business of followers, Gau has had the audacity – and the genius – to promote a unique way of doing business that has made him rich.

"How many people would like to make more money and work less time?" That's the brain-stumper Gau asks at his boot camps. The heart of Gau's philosophy is built around that idea: through time management, heavy appointment booking and niche marketing, you can generate a constant flow of new, affluent clients, stop killing yourself 60 hours a week scraping for new business, and make a lot more money.

A crucial component of Gau's strategy focuses on marketing to a carefully selected niche, in his case, affluent people over 60. And while some of the producers in his firm, Torrance, CA based Kavesh & Gau, accept clients with as little as $100,000 in investable assets, Gau has a $500,000 minimum. He says that he can make as much money on one such account as on 10 $50,000 accounts, while spending less time. Also, older, wealthy people are generally looking for specialists, and know the value of someone like Gau.

Gau is also ferocious when it comes to seminars, both public and private. His firm does seminars year-round, focusing on "confusing the attendees with facts" as Gau puts it. Instead of educating yourself right out of a client, he says, you should present so much information to the people who come to your seminars that they need to meet with you just to get their bearings. He also insists that everyone who wants to meet be booked then and there, at the seminar. "You've got them in front of you, so make the appointment," he says.

In his systematic use of time management procedures, his willingness to "fire" bad clients (also called "trimming the deadwood"), his disdain for cold calling, and his focus target marketing while not trying to be all things to all people, Gau is a perfect example of Personal Marketing principles taken to their utmost extreme. That's why he may be the best-paid financial planner in the United States.

Perception Becomes Reality

How do Joe and Mary Investor generally perceive financial advisors and stockbrokers? For the most part, as money-grubbing opportunists or downright crooks looking to profit from simply throwing someone else's money into a new mutual fund. That's the perception, and as you may have heard, perception is reality. You can't fight a tide of impression and prejudice on your own, and you can't change the general public's impression of your profession.

Fortunately, you don't have to. You only need to change how people perceive you. In fact, a Personal Marketing campaign that sets you apart as a friendly, warm, interesting person who seems like he'd be great to work will benefit you by contrasting you against the general perception of financial advisors. If you come across as the exception to the rule, you're going to be that much more attractive to your prospective clients.

It's All About Differentiation

You see, being different from your competitors in the eyes of your prospects is the most important thing. It's called differentiation, and it's a fundamental marketing principle. Basically, you market yourself by highlighting a set of characteristics – your military experience, your travels, your family's local history, your previous career racing cars, whatever – that make you stand out from the crowd, and then hammer those characteristics home over a period of time through consistent marketing efforts.

Differentiation is the key to rising above "the noise," as marketing pros like to call the din of competing products and companies. In your case, the noise is competing financial advisors, insurance companies, magazines, books, trading and investor advice Web sites, as well as huge wirehouses with globally recognized names. By setting yourself apart, you ensure that prospects won't lump you in with all the others, but will instead see you as unique. That's the key to being remembered.

Resources

The World's Greatest Brands, edited by Nicholas Kochan. 1997, 188 pg., hardcover, published by New York University Press. This great oversized book is a priceless guide to the world's top brands-such as McDonald's, Budweiser, and Disney – and what makes them universally recognized and globally effective at selling products. It's a perfect introduction to the world of branding.

Image Marketing vs. Direct Response
How Both Work Together

You see image marketing everywhere. It's in the heart of all fashion marketing for mega-names like Calvin Klein. It's in the famed "Think Different" commercials running for Apple Computer's iMac. It's all over the strange, evocative ads that pervade youth culture magazines for everything from hip-hop records to athletic shoes. It's image, and it's built by image marketing.

Then you have the other extreme. You see it in a million commercials for kitchen gadgets and special CD music collections. In newspaper ads pitching "this weekend only" sales of late-model autos. In billboards which suggest that you call The Latest Monster Las Vegas Hotel now, from your cell phone. It's direct marketing, image marketing's not so subtle cousin, focused on getting the sale and generating that phone call right now. If image marketing is a suave, soft-toned sales consultant in a muted Armani suit, direct marketing would be Billy Bob in an orange checked blazer and a plaid tie.

You Need Both

Here's the misleading myth: image marketing is only for rich corporations with huge marketing budgets. That's what most marketers, financial companies, and certainly most financial professionals, believe. It's understandable. Image marketing is about the slow crafting of an image in the marketplace, it's not about getting immediate results and sales. Direct marketing, also called "direct response," is all about producing calls, driving customer traffic, and getting immediate revenue in the door. One is about feel and impression, while the other is about "Call Now!" Yet you need both to make Personal Marketing work.

Unfortunately, financial professionals generally think that because image marketing takes time and doesn't generate immediate results, they can't afford it. That's why too many of them fall back on typical ads and direct mail which always end with the same tired sales pitches and "call today for these special tips on which companies will perform in the 21st century stock market" pleas for phone calls. To the consumer, accustomed to receiving such messages daily, they all start to look the same. You can't afford to be lumped in with other advisors in a market where everyone is offering the same services. You must stand out.

A Relationship Starts With an Image

Here's the fundamental thing to remember about image marketing versus direct marketing: image marketing is built around a relationship, direct marketing is built around an offer. That's why all your Personal Marketing work must begin with relationship building efforts before moving onto direct response and offer-based marketing.

Look at it this way. Traditional, corporate-style financial services marketing has always been based around the "call today" model. "Call today" to receive a free portfolio analysis, a free booklet on the stock market, etcetera. But that approach has a major flaw: how is the consumer supposed to know if your offer is worth anything if he doesn't first know who you are? It comes down to trust. Any direct response offer carries much greater weight when the person offering it is familiar and trustworthy to his audience.

Prospects aren't buying from a financial services company, a broker-dealer, an accounting firm or an insurance company. They're buying from you. Your key to success it to hit your prospects with a strong image message, telling them who you are and what you stand for, while your competitors are still selling the same old surface messages. Then, once your image is established, entice your prospects with value-added offers designed to generate phone calls and compel them to action. It's a combination that when used properly can attract more clients than you ever thought possible...and make you a fortune.

A Good Image Repels and Attracts

The most carefully crafted images repel people. When creating your image, keep in mind that your image need not appeal to everyone, only to your target audience. If everyone likes your image, it probably is not emotional enough to attract your target audience. Even the most successful images repel. Look at a movie like Titanic. Even though its spectacularly filmed image of young love aboard a doomed ship raked in over $1 billion worldwide, there are many people who hate the movie. You can't be all things to all people, so don't try. And don't create your image by committee. Decisions by committee are great for marketing strategy and team building, but terrible for crafting creative excellence. This is true for two reasons:

1. It's nearly impossible to get more than two people to agree on anything.

2. Great artists always work alone because creative expression is not rational. It's emotional and no two people can share the same emotion.

It is reasonable for you to want to get an opinion on your image from some people, but be wary of the number of people you ask. The more opinions you heed, the more you'll mute your image.

Glossary

CALL TO ACTION: The phrase at the end of a marketing piece which specifically tells the reader what to do to get in touch with you or take the next step in your relationship. It could be a sentence asking them to "call today" an invitation to a public seminar, or your Web site address.

Emotional Marketing vs. Logical Marketing

It's a debate in marketing circles: do people respond to logical, factual information in marketing and advertising, or do they act strictly based on the emotional impact of a marketing piece. A little of both, to be honest. But when it comes to money, people are much more emotional than they would ever admit. Look at the stock market – a financial juggernaut driven by panic, speculation, and excitement. Hardly a logical enterprise, most of the time. Money is an emotional subject, and your marketing must first touch the emotions of the prospect before any logical information will make an impact.

If this sounds ridiculous, we don't blame you. But think about it. What are the criteria people tend to look for in their relationship with their financial advisor (remember, this is a relationship business)?

- Trust
- A good communicator
- Respects their wishes and needs
- Talks to them as equals

Not one has anything to do with financial expertise. All deal with emotional comfort. That's primarily how people make buying decisions. They like to think they make them based on logic, and sometimes that's true. But more often than not, people buy soft drinks, shoes, clothes, and even cars based on a feeling of emotional comfort and brand familiarity. And you can only build those through image marketing.

The Four Principles of Image Marketing

So we've established that when starting down the Personal Marketing road, image marketing comes first. But what's the essence of image marketing? What makes it effective? As with all marketing, there are rules. Here are the core principles you'll need to grasp and follow about image marketing:

1. It takes time. This might be the hardest to accept. Novice marketers often think that they'll reap dozens of new clients within days of mailing their first new marketing piece. Not with image marketing. It takes time to move the audience through the three levels of image marketing (see below) and get them to the point where they are ready to be receptive to your direct sales message. Image marketing is infiltrative marketing, and the message needs to penetrate in its own good time down to the reader's

consciousness. Think back to our favorite example, Nike. How long did it take before "Just do it" became synonymous in your mind with the shoe company? It takes time.

2. It's not head-on. Head-on marketing would mean that your Personal Brochure would have a cover that showed you holding fistfuls of money with the caption "I'll Make You Rich!" Do you think anyone with an IQ over 65 would believe that? But that's the kind of in-your-face message some financial pros want to use. Image marketing is more sophisticated and less blatant. It uses images and ideas that bring up positive feelings...feelings of curiosity or longing or commonality. A marketing campaign sent to a community of sailboat owners might feature photos of racing yachts and talk in nautical terms, with little mention of investments.

3. It's emotional. Look at Apple's wildly successful line of iMac computers, and the equally successful advertising done by TWBA/Chiat/Day in Venice, California. The entire "Think Different" campaign had nothing to do with computers. Not a word. It was all about making Macintosh buyers feel that if they bought one of the Popsicle-colored CPUs, they'd be joining the ranks of creative rebels like Einstein and Salvador Dali. Apple struck at the emotional chord, and they struck hard. Your image marketing must make an emotional impact on your reader to be truly effective.

4. It costs more. This is what stops most advisors from getting into Personal Marketing. They want instant results, and image marketing is part of a long-term, forward-thinking

marketing strategy. Image marketing costs more than simply sending out a series of "call now" sales letters. It demands quality printing, wide distribution, and repetitive mailing. It entails more work for fewer immediate results. The cost is part of the reason we ask financial professionals to make sure they are ready to commit their time and resources to a Personal Marketing approach before beginning. Generally, the cost of your image marketing will be at least twice the cost of the same amount of direct marketing, and during the first 90 days, it may only produce a fraction of the results, in terms of immediate sales.

So Why the Hell Am I Doing This Image Marketing?

The answer is simple: you're laying the groundwork for your direct marketing to be five to ten times more effective. Think of image marketing as plowing the field: you're breaking up hard topsoil, which consists of jaded consumers who are sick of sales messages from you and your colleagues, with warm, personal, non-sales material that catches them completely by surprise. Then, when the soil is ready, you plant your direct marketing seeds and watch them grow. Without image marketing, you're just dropping seeds where the other guys have, hoping a few will sprout, while the rest get eaten by the crows.

The Three Levels of Image Marketing

1. Awareness

   To work with you, the consumer must first know that you exist. Pretty basic, but you'd be amazed at how many financial professionals forget this simple fact.

   The first job of any image marketing campaign is to create awareness of your name, your profession, your face, and your company in the mind of the consumer. Awareness is easy, typically requiring 2-3 exposures to your marketing message.

2. Knowledge

Once the consumer knows who you are, he must know what you do and what you can potentially offer him. This takes more time, because the consumer must gain awareness of you, then take the time to read your message and understand its meaning. That's why clarity in writing is so critical—you're not there to answer questions. Knowledge of what you do and who you are takes more time than awareness, typically 5-6 exposures to your message or 2-3 complete read-throughs of a quality Personal Brochure.

3. Trust

This is the Holy Grail. Reaching the trust level means that the consumer knows who you are, understands the value of what you do, and sees some common link between you and him, some ground on which you can meet and connect. This is the goal of all marketers, and it's not reached with every consumer. It takes the most time of all, typically 10-12 exposures to your message, several thorough read-throughs of a brochure, or in many cases a brief personal meeting.

Case Study: Discover Online Brokerage

One of the best examples of image marketing for a financial service is the work done for Discover Online Brokerage, the stepchild of the Discover credit card. You've probably seen these television commercials, the one with the big, bearded tow truck driver who "only does this because he likes helping people," and sends the button-downed customer into despair when he confesses that he owns his own island country. Or the spot with the crusty bartender and the smug Yuppies who get their comeuppance when they find out the bartender is a billionaire. It's a great campaign.

For our purposes, here's the key question: What do those TV spots have to do with online trading? Answer: almost nothing. They are pure emotional advertising, intended to make you feel good about using Discover Brokerage. They suggest that you can get ultra-rich trading online, they make you laugh, and only lightly bring up the Discover name. Nothing about system reliability, speed, or features of the Web site. In the first six months of the campaign, traffic at the Discover trading site more than doubled.

1. Direct Marketing: Asking for the Sale

Direct marketing is the second wave of your marketing assault, meant to get prospects in your office, where you can use your sales skills and personal charm to turn them into paying clients. Successful direct marketing is all about knowing the urgent needs of your clients – what marketers call "knowing their pain" – and offering them things that will ease their pain, if only they call you today for more information.

Simply put, direct marketing is the action-oriented counterpart of image marketing. In direct marketing, you're sending your prospect a mailer, brochure or other item in the hopes of eliciting an immediate response-a phone call, an e-mail, or a personal visit to your office. You're looking for the payoff to the trust you've built with your image marketing.

And here's where too many financial professionals fall short. The time for subtlety in marketing is with your image marketing. In direct response marketing, it's time to ask for the business. Asking for the business is one of the great overlooked skills in any marketing approach, personal or otherwise. That's why in Personal Marketing, we recommend the following:

- Be clear. The prospect knows that you're trying to get his business; it's no secret! Be clear about what you want and what you're offering.

- Make the pitch more than "Work with me and I'll show you how to earn 20% a year." That's an empty promise. Be specific. Offer precise tips, named programs for "reducing your tax liability through charitable remainder trusts," and so on.

- Have a plan of action once you get the business. "Um, OK, I'll call you in two weeks to set up a meeting," is not the way to respond once someone hands you their 50 years of financial accrual and says, "Help me." Have materials ready to send in the interim, and set up a firm meeting at the time of your call.

Glossary

Qualified Lead: A prospect who contacts you after having seen your marketing materials, has been referred to you by someone else, or has learned about you in some way and made the decision to contact you. An unqualified lead would be someone who simply sees your ad in the newspaper, reads the number, and calls without knowing anything else.

Direct Marketing Key #1: Candor

Consumers are cynical, low on patience, and largely convinced that anyone making a direct response offer is trying to cheat them in some way. That's a barrier you've got to cross, and there's a way to do it: by being as open, candid and honest in your direct mail as possible.

Don't make gaudy promises in your direct response cards or letters. Don't use hackneyed phrases like "securing your financial future." Instead, talk to your prospect about real things: getting a higher annual return on his mutual fund investments, saving money by going fee-based, benefiting from a third-party money manager, and so on. Instead of talking in vague terms, be specific and very open.

Direct Marketing Key #2: Strong Offers

People need a reason to call, and generally they need something stronger than an offer to sit with you and talk. Some may not need more, but the majority will want added value for spending time with you, at least until they know that you are what you say you are. That's where strong direct response offers come in. In your direct response pieces, offer the prospect something of value for calling, free of charge. Good examples include:

- A "special report" on the stock market
- A subscription to a useful newsletter
- A list of inside tips on choosing mutual funds, insurance, etc.
- Free tickets to a special seminar you're giving
- Free financial software
- A discount on tax preparation services from a local CPA

The point is to offer the consumer value in a way that doesn't obligate him to spend his time. Once you have the prospect on the phone, you can turn on the charm and use those sales skills to set up that all-important personal meeting.

Two Great Tastes That Taste Great Together

Image marketing and direct response marketing are separate approaches that are usually kept separate in marketing tools. But not all the time. It's possible to combine image and direct marketing very effectively, and Personal Marketing does it quite well.

Confused? Picture this: you have a compelling Personal Brochure filled with great photos and information about your passion for mountain climbing and how the sport has taught you about perseverance and striving for excellence. The copy just touches on the fact that you are also a financial advisor specializing in estate and retirement planning. But, on the back of the piece is a special toll-free number that prospects can use to call and receive a special promotional offer, perhaps a Special Report on undervalued stocks.

That's combining image and direct marketing. You'll see it frequently in TV advertising: a wild, dramatic or edgy ad plays without a hint of a sales pitch, and at the very end a phone number dissolves on the screen, with no voice-over or anything else. Combining image and direct marketing is all about the loudness of your sales pitch.

Cover Your Bases All Three Ways

For the most successful Personal Marketing results, build a campaign that features all three marketing approaches:
- Pieces with just an image marketing message
- Pieces with just a direct marketing message
- Pieces combining both messages at the same time

This will give you the most bang for your buck and the best chance of turning prospects into clients.

Resources

- The Complete Idiot's Guide to Marketing Basics, by Sarah
  White. 1997, 428 pg., published by Alpha Books. This part
  of the outstanding "Idiots" series of how-to books is a
  wonderful complement to The Brand Called You. It's a
  more general marketing resource that offers a wide array
  of marketing facts, including information on customer
  behavior and sales tools.

Part II
Personal Marketing Strategy

CHAPTER THREE

Target Marketing
Divide And Conquer

You're standing on a street corner in a busy urban downtown. You're dressed in your best, carrying a huge stack of the latest brochures detailing your financial services. As people walk by, you stop them and try to give them a brochure. Some take it, some politely refuse, some ignore you. But you try to hand one to every person who passes. At the end of the day, you feel as though you've made some progress in building your business.

The Perils of Marketing to Everyone

You just wasted a day of your time. Because almost all the people who took your brochures gave them a quick glance then tossed them in the nearest trash can. Almost no one kept your brochure or really read it. Chances are, you'll get no more than a handful of calls from your day's activity. Why? Because you were marketing to people who didn't care about what you had to say, and who didn't need your services.

Welcome to the world of "horizontal marketing," where advisors try to convert anyone within reach into a client, regardless of their wealth, their location, their ability to provide referral business, or anything else.

Glossary

Target Marketing: The strategy of choosing smaller audiences to receive your marketing message, based on how they fit with your lifestyle, interests, professional skills and/or business development goals.

What is Target Marketing?

Smart financial professionals don't try to turn every warm body into a client. Instead, they locate specific groups of people, select them based on income, occupation, lifestyle or other factors, and then develop marketing strategies designed to appeal just to those groups. This principle is called "target marketing," and it's a fundamental component of Personal Marketing.

Target marketing is "vertical marketing" – tightly focused to appeal to a smaller, well-defined target audience. In a ferociously competitive financial market, target marketing is the only effective way to attract the clients you want and keep your marketing costs under control while having the maximum impact.

Case Study – Kenneth Ready

Target marketing is all about selecting your niche, and few financial advisors have chosen a niche as specialized – or as challenging – as Kenneth Ready. A 19-year industry veteran who works for Prudential Securities' Denver office, Ready handles the financial affairs of nearly 50 National Football League players. This narrow niche audience (he doesn't actively seek any other type of accounts) has thrust Ready into a world of big salaries, limited careers, and high expectations.

"When you niche market, you've increased your risk," says Ready, who began working with pro athletes in 1992. "In a small market like this one, people all know each other. So if you screw up, everyone knows about it." He asserts that with so many financial advisors looking for a piece of the lucrative – and supposedly glamorous – sports market, the only thing that matters is reputation.

"Athletes care about service, about having someone they can trust to do things for them," Ready says. With pro athletes virtually absent from daily life for up to six months a year, their advisor needs to be able to handle all their day-to-day finances, a job which is far more demanding than many reps realize. "Working with one professional athlete is like working with 20-30 regular clients," he says.

Ready won't reveal the specific methods he uses to bring new athletes into the fold. However, he does say that this market "chose him" when an athlete approached him about financial planning. That athlete referred a colleague, and the referral chain grew. The importance of referrals, he says, is why building a reputation is absolutely critical.

And no matter what market you want to target, says Ready, it's just as important to know that market inside and out. "Learn your market and know everything about the people," he states. "If you decide to work only with heart surgeons, you'd better know everything about the heart, including how many times a day it beats."

Why Target Marketing Works

- It allows you to carefully choose the people to whom you market your services, based on their revenue potential, shared interests or background, and how many of your competitors are targeting them as well.

- It allows you to focus your marketing message to a specific group, which lets you appeal strongly to the audience's "hot buttons."

- Its tighter focus lets you get your message to your target audience more often and more consistently, increasing your chances of getting that all-important phone call.

- By choosing a target audience based on your own interests, knowledge or personal background, you'll have a built-in connection with your prospects, communicate with them better, and enjoy working with them.

Benefits of Target Marketing

Target marketing – deliberately excluding potential clients – seems to defy common sense. But does marketing to everyone, with no real plan and no idea if those people will help you reach your goals, make any sense? Target Marketing offers real benefits that make it the only sensible choice for a smart financial professional who wants to turn his practice into a real business:

- The opportunity to dominate a specific market through consistent promotion and image building, locking out most of your competitors.

- The ability to control marketing costs by not sending materials to everyone, but only distributing to a small, lucrative audience.

- A healthier return on investment as you convert a higher percentage of your target prospects for a lower cost.

- The ability to choose a target audience that's custom-tailored to help you meet your goals for income, free time and growth.

Target Marketing Does Defy Logic

Some advisors are reluctant to follow target marketing principles because they seem to go against common sense. It seems logical that to get the most new clients, you need to get your marketing message to as many people as possible. However, that's a sales approach that doesn't take into account the quality of your prospects. Target marketing is all about focusing on quality, not quantity.

We've discovered that the more you reject the kind of business you don't want, the more you will attract the business you do want. You don't want bottom-feeders; you do want affluent families or young couples on their way up. It's as if your marketing is a beam of light. Shine it on a wide area and it has little effect on anything or anyone it touches. But focus it to a narrow beam, and while it won't hit as many people, those it touches will be brilliantly lit. By focusing your marketing on a smaller subset of people who are the kind of clients you want, your marketing becomes stronger.

Choosing Your Target Audience

The most important part of target marketing is choosing your target audience. Choose the right group and exploit them properly and you'll increase your income, reduce the amount of time you spend marketing, and enjoy clients with whom you have something in common.

A target audience can be almost any group, based on anything. However, they do tend to fall in one of three categories:

Geography

- City, State, Zip code, Regions within a city, etc.

- Location-based
  Some financial planners market only to the residents of certain gated communities, or enclaves situated around country clubs.

Client

- Occupation-based
  You'll choose these audiences based on what they do. Teachers, high-tech workers, government employees, or engineers.

- Lifestyle/Hobby-based
  You can choose your audience based on their interest in a lifestyle or hobby that often reflects affluence, such as golf, sailing, collecting classic autos, or travel.

- Age-based
  You can market to young families, retirees, middle-aged couples on their way up, and so on.

- Background-based
  Some advisors choose to market to groups with whom they share a common personal back ground, such as organizations of university alumni.

- Other categories
  You can choose a target audience based on religion, political affiliation, marital status, or many other criteria.

Product or Service
- Financial Planning
- Estate Planning
- Retirement Planning
- Asset Management
- Insurance
- Trading
- Bonds
- Tax Preparation

You'll find specialization by product or service the hardest to do, because every other financial advisor can offer the same products or services as you. The only time you should specialize by product or service is if you have a specialized audience with a specific need, such as a large corporation looking for help managing its employee retirement program.

Which criteria should you use to select your target audience? Trick question: you should use a combination of all three. You should have a defined geographic region, a specific type of client in that region, and have the right products and services for that clientele.

Case Study: The CFP for Engineers

The best target audiences are those which match your personal tastes or experiences. We're familiar with a CFP who works exclusively with mechanical, civil and electrical engineers. A former aerospace engineer himself, he's in an area filled with aerospace and manufacturing firms, giving him ample opportunity to reach his target audience. Engineers don't see him as a salesman, but as a fellow engineer who speaks their language. He knows how to work with them—he loads them with data and information and lets them digest it for 10 days before calling. In the 18 months since focusing only on this target audience, his income has nearly doubled. The funniest thing is, his number one source of new business is referrals from other advisors who either can't or won't work with engineers.

Choose One Target Audience at First

Don't overdo it. Trying to market to too many target audiences is one of the classic blunders. When advisors get cold feet about targeting to a narrow group, they may choose four or five target audiences and try to market to them all simultaneously. This will dilute your efforts and wear you out. We recommend researching and locating as many as three solid target audiences, but ONLY MARKET TO ONE TARGET AUDIENCE FOR AT LEAST ONE YEAR.

Putting all your eggs in one basket is scary, but the most effective marketers do. Can you specialize in financial planning for a whole county and be successful? Sure, but only if your competition is lazy and you have an enormous marketing budget. You'd be shocked at how much money you can make if you simply offer financial planning for medical professionals in one large medical building or complex. The hardest part is making the commitment.

Work With People You Like

Seems simple, but it's the most important factor in choosing your target audience. Work with people you relate to and can enjoy spending time with. If you like your clients, you'll do a better job.

Glossary

Cost Per Lead: This refers to what it costs you (printing, mailing, follow-up and time) to get a prospect in your office. You want your CPL to be as low as possible.

Get the Facts

You start with research. Look at the communities in your area, the industries, the popular hobbies and lifestyles. Be as specific as possible in selecting groups to research; it's better to pick "sailboat owners" than "people who live on the coast."

Once you've chosen groups to examine, you need to find out everything you can about them. The Lifestyle Market Analyst is a great place to start. It's an extraordinary book that breaks down geographic areas of the U.S. by Zip code and provides a huge range of demographic information for each area. Look at the incomes, occupations, locations and other factors of possible groups you want to target. (The Lifestyle Market Analyst is available at some libraries. If you can't get your hands on it, you may call our offices at 888-730-5300 and we'll research your information and fax it to you.)

Once you've done some research into various possible target audiences, ask yourself the following questions about each group:

- Can I offer the services they need?
- Am I comfortable working with these types of people?
- Are they close enough to me geographically?
- Does their income and investment history suggest that I will be able to meet my income goals?
- Are they already deluged with financial services advertising?
- Do they offer the potential for referral business?
- Will I be able to service the clients I might acquire?

Your Target Group

You should end up with a list of potential target audiences that reads like this:

- Homeowners living in the Lost Hills community
- Owners of small businesses in King County
- Faculty and administration at the two area universities

Tailoring Your Services

If your area of greatest expertise is retirement, estate planning, or charitable remainder trusts, marketing to Generation X high-tech workers is not your best option.

Before making a final decision on your audience, look at your services. Can you tailor them to fit the needs of the audience you've chosen? If not, can you take the services that are your strongest and find a target audience that needs them? Keep in mind that tailoring your services isn't just a matter of the services themselves, but also how you communicate them in your marketing materials. We'll cover that in a later chapter.

Scouting the Competition

All's fair in love and war...and business development is war. To know if a target audience is worth pursuing, you've got to know if it's saturated by marketing and sales efforts from other financial advisors, or if it's virgin territory, somehow overlooked by everyone else.

Here are some tactics you can use to get a read on competitive activity within a potential target audience:

1. Talk with people in that audience and ask them if they get a lot of financial advertising. Don't indicate that you're interested in advertising to them, but that you're looking at advertising patterns in their local area. People are more than happy to complain about the advertising they receive, so long as you're not trying to sell them some thing.

2. If you get people on the phone, ask them to send you copies of some of the mailers they've received. This is a great way to get a read on who's marketing and how.

3. Watch local publications, especially those targeting certain communities or groups, such as yacht club papers or corporate newsletters. If you see financial professionals advertising in these publications, call and ask for samples of their materials.

4. Examine your competitors' materials. Are they targeted to the audience you're pursuing, or just written for a general audience? Are they high-quality or second rate? The lower the quality and the weaker the message, the better your chances of moving in on someone else's territory.

So, You've Checked Out the Competition...

Now what? Well, your actions should depend on the situation you've found in that target audience:

1. If your conversations with people reveal that many of them are happy clients of the same advisor, and this advisor's materials are classy and highly professional, forget this audience. Your competitor is too well entrenched and it will cost you too much in time and effort to catch up.

2. If you discover that several advisors are marketing to the audience with some success, but no one is dominating the audience, it's a toss up. If the majority of the marketing tools from the different advisors are high quality, you'll face an uphill battle from multiple competitors. You should probably wait until you're a more experienced marketer.

3. If you find that many advisors are marketing but none has many clients among your audience, then it's likely that no one is doing a stellar job. You'll have competition, but if the audience is lucrative and worthwhile, you should probably try to dominate it.

4. If the audience is under-served or hardly anyone is marketing to it at all, jump! Keep your efforts quiet, but get your marketing program up and running to this audience as fast as possible.

Choosing Your Target Audience

Look at the final list of target audiences that have passed all your tests. Pick the one that's most likely to provide you with the most clients. Worry less about affluence and more about common connections with the people, and how their needs fit with your skills and services. Also, look at the potential for referrals within the audience. Choose that audience as your first target, and put the others aside until you've got more experience.

Get Marketing!

Once you've selected an initial target market that fits your services and goals, it is likely to respond to your marketing message and isn't overrun by competitors, you're ready to get started with your Personal Marketing campaign.

Resources

Here are some resources for finding demographic information about your possible target audiences:

- The Lifestyle Market Analyst – published by SRDS, 800-851-7737
- Municipal Reference Guides – published for major municipalities by National Resource Directories – (800) 242-5511 or www.towndata.com
- Database America – www.databaseamerica. com
- CACI Marketing Systems – (800) 394-3690 or www.demographics.caci.com

CHAPTER FOUR

Positioning
Own A Piece of Your Client's Mind

The mind of your prospect is a vast landscape of file folders, each holding information important to that individual. Some are labeled "Places I Leave My Car Keys," others "Family Birthdays" and so on. For every thought, there's a file. Now look at the file on financial services professionals. Is your name on the label? Is it blank?

Glossary

Positioning: Using marketing materials and consistent marketing efforts to establish a lasting, unique identity for you in the customer's mind. A perfect example is the positioning of BMW as "the ultimate driving machine." A position has little to do with your merits and everything to do with how the customer perceives you.

Determining What's on the Label

Positioning is the art of controlling what goes on the client's mental label. You see, each prospect and client is going to have a mental set of "identifiers" – qualities and images they associate with you. As a savvy personal marketer, you need to control what those identifiers are. By controlling what goes on the label of people's mental files, you can control their perceptions of you. And as a wise man once said, perception is greater than reality.

Why Positioning Matters

You see positioning all the time in consumer products. Soft drinks are positioned as the drink of Generation X snowboarders. Cars are positioned as being in "relentless pursuit of perfection." Computers are positioned as the choice of creative rebels who want to think different. And so on. The marketing of Mountain Dew, BMW, and Apple Computer are perfect examples of position-driven marketing. These companies identified a territory they wanted to occupy in their customers' minds, and set out to capture that territory with consistent messages.

At first glance, positioning doesn't seem to make sense for financial services. Think again. You are selling a product – YOU. And like any product, you have competition that's trying to get noticed by the same people you're selling to. The result is that you get lumped in with all the other financial advisors in the marketplace, and when you're thought of as "just another financial planner," it's nearly impossible to stand out.

Something to Grab

Gateway Computers is a perfect example of how to use positioning to suddenly break out of the herd in the public's perception. For years, Gateway had been making personal computers, and good ones. But they weren't any better known than many of their competitors, and they lagged far behind the top players in the industry.

So what did Gateway do? They went customer-friendly, adopting the cow-patterned packaging and graphics, a down-home attitude about service, and a pride in their non-Silicon Valley South Dakota roots. The result: they suddenly stood out as the "friendly" computer maker with the cute cow boxes, and their sales skyrocketed. Now Gateway is the second-largest direct-to-consumers seller of PCs in the U.S., selling $6 million worth of product over the Internet each day! Gateway recognized an essential of positioning: give the customer a "handle" to grab onto, something instant they can identify you with, and they'll remember you over the competition.

How Do You Use Your Position?

Your position is the starting point for all your marketing work, from the design of your brochure to the tagline on your business cards. Before you decide on what to write or what pictures to use, you need to develop and refine your position. Think of it as the foundation on which the rest of your marketing will be built.

Here's an example:

Rob wants to use Personal Marketing to turn his moderately successful one-man financial planning business into a thriving, multi-person company. Before doing anything else, he works on choosing his target audience. Once he determines this, he starts developing a position.

Rob works near a major international airport, and his chosen target audience consists of the 500 or so pilots and airline personnel and their families who live in the area. Knowing that pilots are often ex-military and have hectic schedules, Rob chooses to construct a position that focuses on his own military career and the efficiency he offers by accessing accounts via the Internet. Eventually, he writes a positioning statement that looks like this:

"The former Navy flier who uses the Internet to offer fast, 24-hour investment advice that maximizes the available time of busy pilots and airline employees."

The public will never see this formal position, but it serves as the basis for all of Rob's marketing. His brochure will feature a dynamic photo of an F-18 in flight, and he'll come up with the tagline "Financial Planning With an Altitude" to use on all his materials.

The Positioning Statement

Positioning is driving a stake in the ground that says what you stand for and how you want your prospects to perceive you. Other examples of strong positioning statements:

- "The corporate retirement specialist who appreciates travel and the finer things in life, and works to help employees and executives enjoy them as well."

- "The Harvard-educated stockbroker who's worked as a corporate executive and turnaround specialist, and is well-equipped to help you choose the right companies for your equity investments."

- "A divorced woman who specializes in helping divorcing couples find mutually acceptable financial solutions, and helps each get back on the road to independent financial growth."

- "The child of the '60s who's a regular volunteer, understands the principles of social responsibility, and helps clients make investments which are socially and Environmentally responsible."

Remember, your positioning statement isn't for public consumption. It's intended to be your marketing bible, guiding all your efforts.

Case Study: Charles Schwab

If there's a study in success in financial positioning, it's Charles Schwab & Company. The nation's largest discount broker, Schwab climbed to the top of the financial services heap by offering low-cost, no-frills service and marketing those attributes relentlessly. Yet when he began in 1971, his company was just another brokerage. The difference was that Schwab and his marketing agency saw the wisdom in differentiating the company based on price. This alienated some of the industry and positioned Schwab out of the high-end, high-margin brokerage business, but they knew there was far more money to be made providing services to mainstream investors.

The key was Schwab's constant marketing blitz. Over years, TV commercials and print campaigns pounded home Schwab's position as "the discount brokerage." At the same time, PR efforts produced story after story about the growing company. The result? A firm that serves more than 5.9 million active investors, controlling more than $542 billion in assets. Most important, Schwab "owns" the discount brokerage position.

Charles Schwab is also an excellent example of Personal Marketing, albeit on a grander scale. He still uses his face and name in TV commercials and print advertising, even though his company hardly revolves around his expertise these days. Why? He's trusted.

Everything Reflects Your Position

After you've printed brochures, sent out direct mail and created a logo and tagline, you must support your position in everything you do. Everything involved with your business is a reflection of your position. If you've positioned yourself as the ultimate efficiency expert, it won't do for prospective clients to arrive at your office only to find it cluttered with boxes, or with your computer on the fritz. By the same token, if you're targeting a high-end, affluent clientele, showing up at appointments in shoddy apparel or a wreck of a car simply makes you look foolish.

Since everything you do will reflect the honesty or dishonesty of your position, it's important to develop a position that's supportable, both in your skill level and your personal presentation. For instance, if you have only a cursory knowledge of corporate retirement planning, but position yourself as a golden parachute expert, you're in for trouble.

Bottom line, your position should not only reflect the needs of your target audience, but your own skills, tastes and lifestyle.

Glossary

SWOT: You'll frequently see this acronym in marketing circles. It stands for Strengths, Weaknesses, Opportunities and Threats – the four criteria used to analyze your business' status in the marketplace.

Just Stick a Target on Your Back...

A good position is like a coveted hill on a battlefield. Sooner or later, somebody's going to try to take it away from the people who possess it. Consumer brands are always playing their own version of King of the Hill, trying to knock each other off the top of the heap. Pepsi pursues Coke, Kellogg's pursues Post, AmeriTrade chases E-Trade.

Once you choose and establish a position that other financial professionals want, you're a target. If you send out direct mail and run newspaper ads proclaiming yourself the "tax killer among retirement planners," and make a ton of money because of it, eventually someone is going to try to move in on your territory.

Protecting Your Position

What can you do to keep your position safe? Here are a few steps:

- Be first. There's no substitute for getting there before the other guy.

- Solicit publications that go to your target audience and get to write articles about your specialty.

- Advertise consistently and aggressively.

- When someone does appear mimicking your position, look for weaknesses in his marketing.

- Build a strong referral base.

Developing Your Position-Step-by-Step

1. Take note of the positions occupied by your competitors.

2. Make a list of the things that make you unique, such as areas of professional expertise, hobbies, your educational background, military service, educational background or where you grew up.

3. Look at your desired target audiences. List each possible audience as specifically as possible – for instance, Married Couples Over 55," "Divorced Women," and "Boat Owners" –and list your attributes that would be most appealing to each. For example, if you're the owner of a sailboat or powerboat, that would obviously appeal to "Boat Owners."

4. Examine the factors that the people in each group use to make buying decisions. Are they more concerned about Cost? Quality? Reputation? Convenience? Experience?

5. Talk to a few current clients to find out how they think about you. Ask them, "What words come to mind when you think of me?" These can be very useful, and might surprise you.

6. Combine your attributes, target audiences, buying factors, and the input of current clients to create a list of important points to be included in your positioning statement.

7. Write a sample positioning statement of 10-20 words. Set it aside for a day or so, then look at it again. Rewrite it if necessary. Does it effectively sum you up? Don't solicit the opinions of your current clients, since the position may be written with a different target audience in mind.

8. Once you write a positioning statement that works, make it the basis for all your marketing.

Resources

- There's no better way to get a handle on the concept of positioning that to read the classic marketing bible that started it all. Positioning: The Battle for Your Mind, by Al Ries and Jack Trout. Despite being published in 1981, it's still the definitive book on positioning, and is available from Warner Books.

- The 22 Immutable Laws of Marketing, also by Ries and Trout, is another indispensable marketing guide, published in 1994 by Harperbusiness.

- The New Positioning: The Latest on the World's #1 Business Strategy is the most recent wisdom on positioning from the gurus of the subject. McGraw-Hill published it in 1997.

So what did Gateway do? They went customer-friendly, adopting the cow-patterned packaging and graphics, a down-home attitude about service, and a pride in their non-Silicon Valley South Dakota roots. The result: they suddenly stood out as the "friendly" computer maker with the cute cow boxes, and their sales skyrocketed. Now Gateway is the second-largest direct-to-consumers seller of PCs in the U.S., selling $6 million worth of product over the Internet each day! Gateway recognized an essential of positioning: give the customer a "handle" to grab onto, something instant they can identify you with, and they'll remember you over the competition.

How Do You Use Your Position?

Your position is the starting point for all your marketing work, from the design of your brochure to the tagline on your business cards. Before you decide on what to write or what pictures to use, you need to develop and refine your position. Think of it as the foundation on which the rest of your marketing will be built.

Here's an example:

Rob wants to use Personal Marketing to turn his moderately successful one-man financial planning business into a thriving, multi-person company. Before doing anything else, he works on choosing his target audience. Once he determines this, he starts developing a position.

Rob works near a major international airport, and his chosen target audience consists of the 500 or so pilots and airline personnel and their families who live in the area. Knowing that pilots are often ex-military and have hectic schedules, Rob chooses to construct a position that focuses on his own military career and the efficiency he offers by

Channel Marketing
The Roads to Your Clients

A channel is any distinct route by which information about you reaches possible clients: networking, advertising, seminars, and so on. The name suggests a canal or a cable, and it's an accurate image; productive channels create a continual flow of information and contacts that produce leads, resulting in a stronger client base. When used properly, marketing channels are your most effective method of generating new business.

What are Marketing Channels?

Any method of getting information to your clients can be considered a marketing channel. The most common marketing channels:

1. Advertising
2. Direct mail
3. Public relations
4. Referrals
5. Seminars
6. Networking
7. Internet
8. "Warm Calling"

Each of these can serve as a conduit for you to reach prospective clients. How you use each one, however, is entirely different. The key to effective channel marketing lies in making one channel support another, making both more effective.

Case Study: Stephen Wolff

Want proof that channel marketing works? Look no further than Stephen Wolff, an RIA operating his practice, First Financial Resources, in Irvine, CA. From $1.5 million in gross dealer concessions in 1997, Wolff grew to $3 million in '98, and has his sights on growing 400%, to $12 million, by 2004. Two reasons for his huge success: he and his associates focus much of their marketing on families who own automotive dealerships, and on selling their estate planning services.

"Because of my specialization in this business I have immersed myself in [the auto dealers'] world and I know their potential financial pitfalls better than they do," says Wolff. Much of First Financial's marketing is directed at the automotive market. Wolff has become a speaker at the National Automotive Dealers Assn. trade show (after exhibiting for years), a major contact point for family-held or closely-held dealerships. The firm also advertises in the industry magazine Automotive News, and has allied itself with more than 60 CPA firms and law firms specializing in auto dealerships.

Wolff has also found that many executives and business owners – the majority of them outside the auto industry – have a great need for clear, intelligent estate planning services. So he conducts numerous public seminars, but recruits the audience very selectively: the room is generally filled with 40-50 multi-millionaires. Wolff is also a member of TEC, The

Executive Committee, a networking think-tank for executives of small and medium-sized businesses. At TEC events and his seminars, Wolff speaks in detail about estate planning for family-owned and closely-held businesses. He comes away from each of these engagements having booked appointments with 30-40% of his wealthy attendees.

Wolff also continually refreshes his marketing materials to his audiences, and tests everything for effectiveness. Sometimes, he says, the most effective tool will be the one he likes the least. "When you go fishing," he says, "you don't bait the hook with what you think tastes good, but what the fish thinks tastes good."

Five effective marketing channels-seminars, trade show exhibits and speaking, direct mail, advertising and networking—plus the prospects for 400% growth. That would taste good to anyone.

Have Five Ways to Reach Your Prospects

It's easy to see why Stephen Wolff is successful. He has six different ways to get to his target audience: trade show exhibits at car dealer conferences, speeches at dealer conferences, direct mail, CPA referrals, articles in trade publications and ads in the same trade publications. No wonder he owns his specialized target audience!

If you want to virtually guarantee success in tapping any target audience for business, develop at least five channels you can use to reach them. Channels work beautifully and synergistically when combined. Think about how you make a decision to purchase a new product. Do you hear about it from only one source? No. You see a TV ad for it, hear about it on the radio, and get a good word from a friend before you even consider buying. Take the same approach with your business. The more channels that communicate your message to potential clients, the more successful you'll be.

Think Campaigns

Too often, advisors think in terms of single channels working by themselves. For example, an advisor will put in many hours preparing a public seminar with the intention of signing up many new clients. But when you ask him about cross marketing with multiple channels, he'll look at you blankly. To get the best results from your channels, you must think in terms of channel campaigns.

That means forgetting the "magic bullet" approach and combining channels to hit the same target audience with the same message from multiple directions. For example, you're having a public seminar. At it, you hand out copies of your Personal Brochure. But you also promote the seminar on your Web site, make the content of the seminar the focus of one or two direct mail pieces, and get the local newspaper to run a short story on the event. In this way, you're not only cross-promoting your seminar, but you're also selling prospects on the seminar information in multiple ways. That's the way to have prospects remember you.

Glossary

Continuity: A common "look and feel" between all your marketing tools. Your brochures, mailers, Web site, business cards, etc. must have the same colors, typefaces, graphics, slogans, and so on. Continuity makes you appear highly professional.

Two Types of Marketing Channels

1. Inclusive—you don't have a lot of control over who sees your message, so you'll likely pull in a larger number of prospects but of varying degrees of quality.

2. Exclusive—you control who sees your message, so you'll attract a smaller number of prospects, but they will probably be of higher quality.

Inclusive channels are Advertising, Public Relations, and the Internet. Exclusive channels are Direct Mail, Referrals, Networking, and sometimes Seminars. A strong channel marketing strategy blends both inclusive and exclusive channels.

Advertising

Print ads in newspapers and magazines. Billboards. Radio and television commercials. Any time you pay for space or airtime used to get your message out to a wide audience, that's advertising. It's a risky way to spend your marketing budget, but also the best way to get your name and position known by the general public.

Why it works: Advertising is hands-off, so once you place your ad, all you do is field calls and follow up. It's a great complement to more time-intensive channels like networking. It also has a wide reach. Placing one ad in a 50,000 circulation local paper can give you more exposure in a week than you've gotten in your entire career.

Why it's risky: Advertising is very inclusive, so you may get a great many unqualified leads. Also, creating ads that "pull," or generate calls, is not as easy as it looks. If you're not careful, you can spend thousands of dollars on ineffective ads.

Direct Mail

Direct mail is exclusive, because you have complete control over who receives it. Direct mail is one of the two most important Personal Marketing channels (the other being referrals) because it allows you to customize your message for your target audience and pre-qualify prospects.

Direct mail may also be the most misused marketing channel. That's due to the "sending anything is better than sending nothing" concept, which is completely false. The direct mail channel is high-maintenance, requiring adherence to a regular schedule and a constant supply of effective new messages.

Why it works: Direct mail gives you a cost-effective way to maintain contact with your clients and prospects, ask for referrals, promote your business, and let people know what you're up to.

Why it's risky: Most people are inundated with junk mail these days, and even the best direct mail risks being lumped in with a pile of credit card offers and dumped in the trash without ever being seen.

Public Relations

PR involves working with the local media to generate coverage of you, your business, and your activities. For the most part, that means issuing regular press releases about the things you're doing-seminars, awards you've won, timely new services you're offering, and so on. If you can put out press releases that appear professional, and cultivate relationships with local editors, you can be the subject of articles, have your speaking appearances covered by reporters, and become an editorial source for financial stories. But it takes time and diligence.

Why it works: PR is objective advertising. People read an article about you, or see you quoted in a feature, and they assume there's no vested interest on the reporter's part. You gain instant credibility – and trust – that's impossible with advertising.

Why it's a risk: PR is time consuming. You can spend hours talking on the phone with editors, writing releases and pitching column ideas, and you might still get nowhere.

Referrals

Nothing gets you in the door like a personal referral. You can actively generate referral business by exploiting this marketing channel.

This essence of using this channel is simple: ask for the business. If you are providing high quality service and keeping your clients happy, they will want to refer their friends and colleagues to you, because they want those people to benefit from your skills and knowledge. Of course, you must provide top-notch service to engender that kind of loyalty and goodwill.

Exploit the referral channel by developing a direct mail program that both asks for the referral and provides materials for clients to pass along. In some cases, offering incentives such as gift certificates is a great way to get clients to drop your name. In any case, don't sit around waiting for referrals.

Why it works: Referrals give you the highest possible quality of lead-people who have already gotten a positive impression of your work from a person they trust.

Why it's risky: If you do it badly, soliciting your clients for referrals can seem like harassment, alienating them and killing your chances for any referral business.

Seminars

Conducting seminars takes time, planning and experience; consequently, it's something you'll probably want to wait on until you're a more experienced marketer. However, when you're ready, conducting either public or private seminars is an outstanding way to reach your target audience.

Public seminars are advertised in your local community or for a specific target audience. They are usually free, and in return for your 90-minute presentation on retirement planning or online investing, you can ask attendees to take away a copy of your brochure. Some financial advisors conduct public seminars once per month.

Private seminars are generally held for corporations or organizations like Chambers of Commerce, and follow the same principles as public seminars. However, institutional audiences may be more demanding, and turning seminars into sales may take much longer than with individuals.

Why it works: You have face-to-face time with your prospects, allowing you to impress them with your personality, knowledge, or professional marketing materials. Seminars also give you a vehicle for generating press coverage, and if you develop an impressive resume as a speaker, you can even start charging for appearances at corporations or financial industry events.

Why it's risky: Setting up seminars takes a lot of time-arranging for a space, advertising, creating educational materials, setting things up on the night of the event, and so on. If it's not effective, you can waste a lot of hours.

Networking

Networking involves making contact with colleagues in businesses which complement your financial practice-real estate, mortgage lending, accounting, estate or tax law, banking, and so on. You can extend networking further by working to make contacts with various important local corporations, Chambers of Commerce, politicians and political parties, and members of the media.

Why it works: Networking lets you make friends and create camaraderie and trust with people who can help you – and whom you can help in return. Remember, the best networking relationships involve mutual benefit.

Why it's risky: Do it badly, and you can turn people off. It's important to resist the temptation to treat people as nothing more than resources to grow your business. To be successful, you must offer a benefit to them, not just come across like you want something.

Internet

Online stock trading is skyrocketing, and more and more consumers are conducting research into companies, mutual funds, and financial firms on the Web. The Internet is a hotbed of financial information, and it can't be overlooked as a marketing channel.

There are several ways to exploit the Internet as a channel:

- Your own Web site—Simply putting your personal and service information online can extend your position into cyberspace and make you appear to be on the cutting edge.

- Direct e-mail—By allowing people to enter their e-mail addresses on your site, you can develop a database of prospects and send them regular news via e-mail for next to nothing.

- Online editorial—With so many financial Web sites, there's an ongoing need for financial articles and columns. If you feel comfortable writing and can sell an online "e-zine" or newsletter, you can put your words before millions of potential readers.

Why it works: The Internet is becoming the financial resource for millions of Americans. Having a presence online enhances the perception of you as a successful, savvy financial professional, and gives prospects a 24-hour, pressure-free way of finding out more about you.

Why it's risky: It's not enough to build a Web site; you've got to advertise it to let people know it's out there. And because less than 25% of the population are Internet users, your audience will be limited.

"Warm Calling"
Bottom line – cold calling is a waste of your time. Calling prospects that don't know who you are is one of the most

odious tasks in business, and it's a pure selling tactic. You can do better. "Warm calling" is calling prospects that have already received your direct mail, come to your seminar, or learned about you in some other way. They know who you are and what you do, and have already formed an opinion about you.

Why it works: Warm calling adds a personal touch and a human voice to your prior marketing efforts, and gives you the chance to make a lasting impression, answer questions, and make the pitch for a personal meeting.

Why it's risky: Some people simply hate to be called, but they will likely never become your clients, anyway. The main risk of warm calling is that it will waste your time if you try too hard to sell your prospect.

Putting Marketing Channels to Work

We could write an entire book on channels. But chances are, you already use many of them, and know some of the tricks to making them work. Here are some more suggestions:

Direct Mail

- Be consistent and persistent.

- Write messages that appeal to emotions and people's sense of humor.

- Use your brochure as a direct mail tool to augment other tools, and track your results.

- Update your materials regularly with new photos, Web addresses, etc.

Advertising

- Place ads designed to get people to call for your Personal Brochure.

- Cross-promote in your ads by always listing your Web address or mentioning your series of direct mail cards.

- Use ads to promote public events such as seminars.

Referrals

- Ask for referrals from current clients.

- Create special materials to send to referred clients, introducing yourself and reminding them how you learned about them.

- Create incentives for clients who refer their friends.

- Establish procedures for you and your staff to treat referral clients like gold.

Publishing/PR

- Learn and follow standard press release format; submit releases once per month, no matter what.

- Meet local editors and establish relationships.

- If you have a column idea, hire a ghostwriter to produce it.

- Send letters to editors, establishing yourself as a source for financially related stories.

Seminars

- Promote seminars through local advertising and flyers on display in public buildings.

- Have educational materials and other "take-aways" to give out at your seminar.

Internet

- Make your Web site a hub for accessing a wide range of financial information. Provide links to major trading sites, financial news sites, and financial firms.

- Hire a professional Web developer to design and create your site.

- Cross-promote your site through all your materials by putting your "www" address everywhere.

- Promote your site to technically aware prospects and clients.

Networking

- Join professional groups where you will meet financial professionals like CPAs, tax attorneys, and bankers.

- Carry brochures to hand out to those expressing professional interest.

- Write a follow-up schedule for contacting colleagues who have expressed interest in using or referring your services.

- Create an incentive program for CPAs, attorneys and others who refer you, and promote the program via direct mail.

General Channel Marketing Tips

- Cross-promote your channels. Put your Web address in press releases; refer to your advertising in your direct mail; hand out invitations to your seminar at a networking event. Use each channel to also promote at least one other.

- Make sure your tagline, logo, and photo are consistent throughout all your channels.

- Don't commit to too many channels. Limit yourself to actively exploiting no more than five, at least at the beginning. For a Personal Marketer just starting out, a good combination is Direct Mail, Networking, Referrals, Warm Calling, and Internet.

Resources

- Chambers of Commerce are perhaps your best source for local networking, mailing lists, seminar audiences, and more. Get more information on your local Chamber and those in your region by contacting the United States Chamber of Commerce, (202) 659-6000 or www.uschamber.org.
- LeTip is a national organization dedicated to helping local business people gain referrals and network to grow their businesses. There are local chapters throughout the U.S. Reach LeTip at (800) 25-LETIP or at www.letip.com.
- Seminar Selling by Paul Karasik. A useful reference for advisors looking for insight on building their business by conducting seminars. 1995, 236 pg., published by Irwin Professional Publishing.

Part III
Personal
Marketing
Tools

CHAPTER SIX

Personal Brochures
The One Tool You Must Have

We've stated it before, but it bears repeating: you are your most important product. So what do you have to promote yourself? You have company brochures to promote your company and a prospectus to promote each product...but this is Personal Marketing. What promotes YOU? The answer, and the foundation of any successful Personal Marketing campaign, is a high quality, client-generating Personal Brochure.

It's a Prospecting Tool, Not a Sales Tool

If all your personal brochure does is get your perspective clients to like you, trust you and have a positive emotional disposition towards you, it has done its job. That's it. A Personal Brochure is a tool for attracting clients, for developing your image and establishing your position with your target audience. It's not a selling tool. It exists to differentiate you from your competition and to tap into the prospect's emotions. It will not, by itself, make your phone ring off the hook.

Most of the brochures we have seen in the financial services industry look the same. They have an ugly black and white "mug-shot" on the cover, talk about nothing but products and services, barely mention the advisor except in a short bio, list their credentials and do nothing but bore prospects to tears. A Personal Brochure is a completely different league of marketing sophistication, one you're ready for.

Glossary

Differentiation: A fundamental of marketing, this is the process of setting yourself apart from your competition by promoting things that make you different from them. Such differentiators may be experience, your personal background, or even the fact that you are savvy enough to have a Personal Brochure.

Your Best Rapport Builder

Do you like your best clients? Do your best clients like you? This is a business of relationships, and building rapport begins before you even meet the client. It begins with your Personal Brochure. A good brochure begins building trust immediately. Once you start working with a new client, you enhance that trust by performing as promised. Then you can deliver your true service: advice. If a client does not trust you, you'll have to debate and argue every recommendation you make. Rapport and trust must begin with the image building materials you send into the marketplace. They are a reflection of you.

Say you meet someone at a cocktail party. Talk about your credentials, how much money you make, or your degrees and designations, and you'll be talking to yourself. On the other hand, converse about where you live, your hobbies, or where your kids go to school, and you may find yourself building relationships. You see, at the outset, all relationships are based on commonality: shared interests, similar backgrounds, etc. You won't share common ground with every prospect, but by telling your personal story in your Personal Brochure, you have the chance to connect with those who have something in common with you.

Five Steps to Creating a Great Personal Brochure

In working with thousands of financial advisors – and designing hundreds of Personal Brochures – we've learned what makes a great brochure. Many of our clients track the results of mailing and handing out their brochures and report their findings back to us. This allows us to know – not theorize or guess – what works best. The following tips are the accumulation of our best advertising theory and proven, practical application.

Step One: Pick a Single, Focused Benefit

You can't be all things to all people. Painting a picture of yourself as the advisor who does everything will only confuse your prospects. If you try to be the advisor who is a great money manager, is Internet-savvy and also offers the best retirement planning advice, you'll just end up with a brochure that's a blunt instrument, not the marketing scalpel it should be. Based on your positioning statement, select one specific benefit to entice your target market. The most effective Personal Brochures are built around a compelling story, and communicate their central benefit in an anecdotal way that works into the story. When selecting your benefit, keep these questions in mind:

- What single benefit is most important to your potential clients?
- What can you share about yourself, which will drive this point home?

Step Two: Write a Personal Biography

Regardless of what you sell-financial services, real estate financing or widgets-if you can't sell yourself, your products will sit on the shelf. By the time a prospect finishes reading your Personal Brochure, he should feel as if he really knows you, as though he has something in common with you. Don't be afraid to share your personality. By revealing yourself as a human being rather than talking about your accomplishments as a salesperson, you can get past sales resistance and make an emotional connection with the reader.

Your personal biography should comprise 75 to 95% of the brochure's content. Don't even mention your professional services for the first two paragraphs. This is a soft sell, and a new sell, and the person is more important than the product. If you throw a hard sales jab in the opening paragraph, the reader will run for cover.

Limit company and service information to one or two paragraphs at most. Present your company as a support system and capitalize on the power of your company name. The link between your image and your established company name increases your credibility in the minds of potential consumers. If you feel you must include your products or services, use bullet points on the back of the brochure.

Case Study: Paul Escudero

Paul Escudero, a financial advisor with Orange Capital Management, Inc. in Orange, CA, has used his Personal Brochure to supercharge his rate of converting prospects into clients. He began using the brochure in January, 1998 at his firm's seminars on money management for seniors. When people attended, they received a packet of information about the speakers, products, and so on. Paul included his Personal Brochure in that packet.

"Out of 50 couples who would attend a seminar," Escudero says, "maybe 40% would sign up as clients. Once I started using the brochure, that jumped to 60%." Escudero uses the brochure in his First Call Kit, a package of information he sends to new prospects, and provides extra copies to give out to referrals.

He knows why the brochure has worked so well. "Retired people like having a warm feeling about a financial advisor. They want to feel like they know you," he says. "With my brochure they know my background, my history, they see pictures of my family, and that gives them that feeling. Plus, the high quality gives them the impression that I've been around a while."

The bottom line? Before using the Personal Brochure, Escudero was doing about $200,000 a year in business. In the first half of 1999 alone, he did nearly $400,000.

Step Three: Some General Writing Guidelines

Use the third-person objective point of view in writing the text. So, instead of "I went to the Air Force Academy," you'll write, "Tom excelled at the Air Force Academy." Consumers associate third-person writing with objectivity, not ego. Keep the text positive – do not mention financial icebergs or bleak scenarios that may frighten the reader.

- Present your material in paragraphs. Salespeople don't always believe in narrative, but most of us prefer to read a good story, and narrative text outperforms short text every time in marketing research studies. Use bullets sparingly as they can interrupt the flow of ideas.
- Be candid and avoid cliches. Consumers are much more sophisticated than ever before, and they have strong "B.S. detectors." Be candid and honest about the realities of life and investing, rather than falling back on cliche phrases and empty promises.

- Use subheads. These short headlines which come before each new paragraph break up the text of your brochure and make it much more appealing to the reader.

Step Four: Create a Knockout Cover and an Appealing Layout

Your brochure must have a compelling cover. The most riveting personal biography or the most exciting presentation of your business philosophy is meaningless if your prospects don't pick up your brochure to begin with. The cover must stimulate a reader's curiosity, crying loudly and unmistakably, "Pick me up!" A casual reader examines the cover, but a curious reader opens the brochure. Do not place any images or text on the cover which refer directly to your company, products or services. Your cover should not sell, but create curiosity. Always place your personal or company logo and contact information on the back of the brochure.

Your personal brochure design should also be appealing and lead the reader into the text. One way to do this is by employing lots of open or "white" space. Too many non-designers feel like they must fill up every inch of space with something. Don't fall into that trap. Densely formatted blocks of text intimidate, and excessive graphics lead readers away from your message. Design is about communication and spacing. Well-chosen images and inviting text will communicate class and professionalism.

Here's an axiom you should never forget: on first glance, the look and feel of your brochure must convey more about your image than any words inside. Great design fosters instant credibility.

Large formats attract more attention, so use a brochure size that stands out. Unusual-sized brochures dramatically increase readership rates. The best shape for brochures is usually a square. One reason is simply because square brochures are different and more likely to be looked at. Also, we associate square materials with invitations. The most effective brochure sizes tend to be 6"x 6", 7"x 7", or 8"x 8" size when folded.

Step Five: Pay For High-Quality Typesetting & Printing

It's essential to use four-color (full-color) printing when producing your marketing materials. Full-color design dramatically increases readability and overall impact, and makes you appear successful and professional.

Good typesetting counts; even the best laser printer will not give you the type quality you need to produce a good brochure. Most printers offer typesetting services at the rate of $150 to $250 per page. It's money well spent. Generally, do not choose the printer who offers you a rock-bottom price. In printing, you definitely get what you pay for. Check to make sure your printer uses a four-color press printing at 175 line-screen or higher, and make sure you see printed samples of his work. Print your brochure on a heavy, high-quality paper; this will ensure good ink absorption and a substantial, quality feel. We recommend 100 lb. gloss cover stock.

Finally, set your type in serif fonts (like the type in this book), 9 to 12 point size. This is shown to be the most readable style of type for people of all ages.

Brochures for Debra Quackenbush and Sarkauskas & Associates demonstrate the uniquely personal character of a quality Personal Brochure. Each brochure attracts certain types of prospects while it repels others. Note the "personality" contained in each brochure. What would your Personal Brochure look like?

The Cornerstone of your Marketing

Conceiving, writing, designing, revising and printing your Personal Brochure will take from 50 to 100 hours of your time. It is time very well spent. The process of creating a strong, compelling, attractive Personal Brochure will also lead you to create your personal slogan and position and choose your target market, the other key components of your marketing campaign. Most important, you'll have an outstanding marketing tool that should serve as the heart of all your future Personal Marketing work.

Nine Uses For Your Personal Brochure

1. Mail to Current Clients

   Mail two copies to all current clients; one for them to keep and one for them to pass along to someone who needs your services.

2. Mail to Prospective Clients

   Mail to any prospective clients.

3. Give Copies to Referral Sources

   Send at least 12 copies to any referral sources such as CPAs and attorneys, with a recommendation to forward the brochure to their clients.

4. Use for Client Maintenance

   Use as part of your "Twelve-Month Drip Marketing Plan" on page 126.

5. New Client Generation

   Use as part of your "Six Week Marketing Blitz Client Generation Plan" on page 129.

6. Networking/Business Card substitute
Hand out at public events, speaking engagements, and networking opportunities. Hand it out in every situation where you would normally hand out a business card. If it's too big to carry, get contacts' business cards and send them a brochure as you return to your office.

7. Public & Private Seminars
Hand out to everyone who attends your seminar, prior to your presentation.

8. Press Kits
Include in press kits or with story submissions you send to editors.

9. Alternative Sources
Advertise in car wash kiosks, place in Chambers of Commerce, Visitors' Bureaus, etc.

Resources

- Communication Arts – One of the leading design magazines in the industry, this beautiful periodical will show you what's being done in designing great collateral materials. You can also find it at www.commarts.com.

- Print – Another leading journal looking at outstanding print design in ads, brochures, packaging and more. Online at www.printmag.com

- Online stock photo resources – Discover the kind of stock images available to you for designing your brochure. The best include PhotoDisc (www.photodisc.com), Tony Stone Images (www.tonystone.com) and Corbis (www.corbis.com).

Personal Postcards Direct Mail Weaponry

Direct mail is the most abused, most misunderstood, and most underutilized marketing tool among today's financial advisors. When managers declare that "direct mail fails," you can almost guarantee that they gleaned such evidence from sending out boring, intimidating or indistinguishable direct mail.

The world's greatest marketers know that when used correctly, direct mail is the best business generating tool available, especially when combined with personal contact. Direct mail can increase your direct contact results by 300-500%. Successful use of direct mail has two secrets: designing mailing materials that appeal strongly to your target audience, and consistent, repetitive mailing over a period of months.

Direct Mail DOES Work

There's a fallacy that direct mail is ineffective. The reason for that belief is simple: most people don't use direct mail properly.

Most advisors who use direct mail do the following:

- Send a letter on company letterhead, sealed in a #10 business envelope.

- Send this letter out to 2,000 people once, with no repetition.

- Do little or no follow-up and receive few, if any, phone calls.

- Conclude that direct mail doesn't work.

That's an unscientific conclusion at best. If direct mail doesn't work, why is our mailbox bursting with it every day? Record clubs, catalogs, credit card offers, and so on—direct mail is a $25 billion annual business in the U.S. because it does work, when you know how to do it right. Master direct mailers know the secrets of effective direct mail: differentiation, multiple mailings, and continuity. And they know how to use them.

Repetition is Critical

Direct mail has one destination: the trash can. That's where 99% of it goes within the first 60 seconds after it's received. No matter how brilliant your Personal Postcard, there's nothing you can do to change that fact. It's a law of direct mailing. That's why repetition and consistency are so important to success.

By sending out direct mail pieces according to a regular schedule, you breed familiarity in your target audience. They come to expect your mailers, even if they don't read them. And by using a consistent design, theme and style of message, you reinforce your identity so that, in spite of themselves, recipients become familiar with your name, your face, and your logo. Eventually (and it can take weeks or months) people learn who you are and what you stand for. That's the kind of familiarity that results in phone calls.

Introducing The Personal Postcard

We're going to share with you the most powerful, versatile direct mail tool ever to hit the financial services field: the Personal Postcard. Personal Postcards are the inseparable companions of the Personal Brochure; together, they're the engine of your marketing machine.

Personal Postcards are the quickest and most cost-effective way of sending regular marketing messages through the mail to prospects. Your card can become a client newsletter, a bulletin of financial opportunities, or a reminder of your services. Personal Postcards gives you an attractive, full-color mailing vehicle to communicate your message to clients and prospects. At the same time, they maintain design and thematic consistency with your Personal Brochure, one of the keys to building a professional marketing image. Finally, using a Personal Postcard allows you to set up a hands-off direct mail program that can be implemented in your absence.

What is a Personal Postcard?

Personal postcards are "shells," oversized (6" x 9" all the way up to 8 1/2" x 11") postcards with a full-color design on both sides, but with a large blank space on one side where a different message can be imprinted with each mailing. On one side, you'll have graphics, your logo, some brief descriptive text about you, and space for mailing information. All will match the content of your Personal Brochure.

On the other side, you'll have one or more color photos and a large space where the message of your choice can be overprinted, usually in 24 hours. Simply write your message, take the card to a commercial printer, and have the message overprinted in black ink on the card. Instantly, you have a customized, full-color mailer! The benefit of such a card should be clear: you can change your message any time to fit the time of year, market news, or any other need, while still sending it on a slick, professional, high-quality mailer.

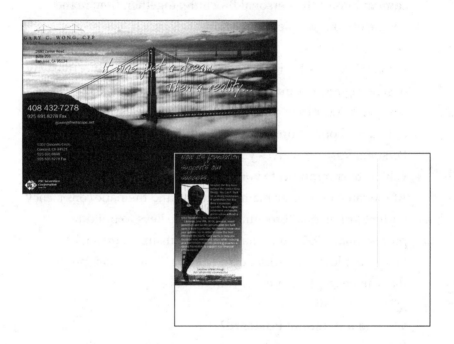

An example of a quality Personal Postcard for Gary Wong, a San Francisco-based advisor. Note that the card allows ample space for customization while capturing the flavor of the region and Gary's personal style.

Designing Your Personal Postcard

Personal Postcards are the backbone of your direct mail system. A Personal Postcard must meet two objectives: build name recognition, and establish a positive emotional disposition towards doing business with you.

Your first objective is to build name recognition, so you must clearly promote yourself – not your company – on your card. Your name and image must be recognizable at a glance. Don't expect people to read your card to find out who you are. They won't.

Second, your Personal Postcard must reflect quality and professionalism by its look and feel. The immediate impression your Personal Postcard makes with its weight, its gloss and the quality of its images will have a greater effect on a prospect's state of mind that the writing or graphics. If your Personal Postcard is well designed but printed on thin and flimsy stock, you will ruin your chances of impressing prospects. Always print Personal Postcards in full-color, on the same stock you use for your Personal Brochure, 100-lb. gloss cover stock.

Personal Postcard Mock-up

Large Formatted Photo - Same as Personal Brochure

Front

Personal Logo

Stamp Indicia

Return Address

Label Space

Contact Information

Company Logo

Large Blank Space

Back

Personal Photo

T _____
_____
_____
_____
_____
_____
_____
_____
_____

Phone Number

Mailing Your Personal Postcard

Once your postcard is printed, you must mail it. First you'll need a mailing list for your target audience. You could compile your own from local information directories, but you'd be wasting time better spent servicing your clients. A better option is to purchase a mailing list from one of many national mailing lists companies (see Resources at the end of this chapter). These companies can provide you with updated lists ready to work with your mail/merge software.

Once you have your list and your cards, you have two choices for mailing: do it yourself or hire a mailing house to do it for you. If you mail yourself, you're again spending a lot of time but saving money. For a smaller mailing sample, such as 500 homes, this is what we'd recommend.

For larger mailings, such as 2,500 recipients, consider a mailing fulfillment house, which will print your labels, stick them on your cards, bundle your cards and get them in the mail for you for a reasonable fee. Many larger printers provide such services, and you can also find mailing houses in the Yellow Pages.

One final ingredient you'll need: a Bulk Rate permit. This permit is printed on your cards and lets you mail to specific Zip codes for about one-third the first-class rate. It's a great money-saver. Get Bulk Rate information from your post office.

Case Study: Titan Value Equities

Titan Value Equities, an independent broker-dealer in Irvine, CA, faced a dilemma. Like many independent firms, they relied on a constant flow of new, top-producing advisors to fuel revenue growth. But as we all know, the recruiting business in financial services is cutthroat. The solution: a creative, strategic direct mail campaign.

Titan designed a six-card direct mail campaign focused on six "bottom line" statements about being a successful advisor. The cards talked about technology, training, payouts and more, and portrayed Titan as the leader in everything. The firm sent out one card per week for six weeks to thousands of independent reps at broker-dealers around the U.S.

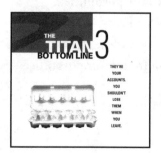

The results were extraordinary. From this campaign, Titan added more than 30 new top producing financial professionals to its team. Ultimately, the growth of Titan Value Equities led to its acquisition by Mutual Service Corporation.

Save Money on Printing

The key to issuing a high quality, economical Personal Postcard is to design a master that you can have preprinted in quantities of at least 5,000; we recommend 10,000. Include a large blank space to overprint timely messages at your local 24-hour printer. Now you've got a full-color template for news, tips and all variety of messages.

Five Types of Personal Postcard Messages

Once your full-color shell postcards are printed, it's an easy matter to have your customized messages overprinted before you mail. Simply write your new message, limiting yourself to a strong headline and 75-125 words if possible. Then take enough cards for your mailing to a "quick print" shop like Sir Speedy, where they can run your cards through their press and generally produce the finished product for pennies per card.

Following are five types of Personal Postcard messages:

Advertising Messages

Turn your Personal Postcard into advertising by printing your company-generated or company-approved advertisements directly onto your card. Most companies generate hundreds of pre-approved ads for their advisors to use, so take advantage of them. Integrate product-driven messages with your personal marketing image, and you'll leave a strong impression in your clients' minds.

Example

When You're 70, Will You Be Living With Your Kids?

Whether it's 10 years down the road or 35, retirement is coming. Will you have enough money to continue the lifestyle you've created, or will you be forced to cut back, maybe even accept help from your loved ones? Starting 10 years too late on your financial plan can set you back for the rest of your life.

Now's the time to start planning for your post-work independence. With my programs designed for many different types of retirement goals, I can get you started with a tax-deferred investment plan that will give you secure, steady growth for decades. If you'd like to invest and then forget about your money while its grows, talk to me soon. I might be able to show you how to create the retirement you've always dreamed of.

Call Ron Johnson today for more information at (714) 555-5555.

Personal Messages

At regularly scheduled intervals, print a personal message on your Personal Postcard to help build the "friendship factor." You want your clients to feel comfortable calling you, and periodic personal messages imply personal consideration. Personal messages can be musings on your kids starting school, a look at an historical landmark that's about to be restored, a story of personal triumph about you or someone else, and so on. Mail personal message cards once per quarter.

Example

Little League. Big Lessons.

My son fell in love with little league last week. Eight years after he was born and fourteen years after my last bleacher tan at Anaheim Stadium. And unexpectedly, I too fell in love with the game again, and I think learned as much as he did. On a little dirt diamond filled with scurrying feet and adventuresome ground balls, numerous ventures were attempted. Bunts. Double plays. Stolen bases. Hit-and-runs. When they worked, it was because the team took wise counsel. Give people a good coach and you'll be amazed at what they achieve – whether the game is baseball or the bond market.

I just wanted to share this with you because I saw how a coach can make the difference – between a single and a strikeout, between success and frustration. I coach some very special "teams" – families who want financial winning streaks. I offer my number – 555-1234 – and some highly experienced advice on the nature of the game that is the investment market. Call for my "Yield of Dreams" brochure that explains why stocks are still first in the financial standings. You'll be glad you did.

Call Ron Johnson today for more information at (714) 555-5555.

Season's Greetings

Use familiar holidays to spice up your regular Personal Postcard. In the card's blank section, overprint a holiday-oriented message. Account for Christian and Jewish holidays, as well as national holidays like Memorial Day and Dr. Martin Luther King Day. Sending holiday postcards not only breaks up the routine of advertising messages, but reminds your clients that you are not only a valuable financial resource, but more importantly, a human being.

Example

While we're celebrating our independence, why not take a step towards yours?

July 4th commemorates the signing of the Declaration of Independence, surely one of the greatest documents in the history of mankind. But if a nation can be independent, why not you and your family? Do you dream of retiring at 50 and traveling, opening your own business, or just having enough money to maintain an elegant lifestyle?

There's a way to get there. It's called financial planning. I can help. Call me at my office soon and let's set up an appointment. I'll show you how smart investing and foresighted planning can give you the independence you've dreamed of.

Call Ron Johnson today for more information at (714) 555-5555.

Newscards

Too many advisors waste tons of time, money and energy producing a four or eight-page newsletter. Instead, turn your Personal Postcard into a Newscard by overprinting an article into the blank space. And here's another way you can get an advantage over your competitors: choose articles specifically suited to your target audience. Most advisors send generic articles that rarely relate to their audience; by sending targeted articles, you gain goodwill and readership.

Example

It looks like interest rates are going up. What will that do to your investments?

As you know, the Federal Reserve Board is going to raise interest rates shortly. As it always does, a rate hike will depress stock prices for a time, but not forever. Do you know how to best take advantage of the market's reaction to a rate increase? Do you know what it means for you in the bond market? I can enlighten you and show you how rising interest rates don't have to put a damper on your investing. Call me today and I'll explain.

Ron Johnson (714) 555-5555

Web Marketing Messages
Highlight features on your Web site to compel readers to visit it.

Example
How Much Money Do You Need To Retire?

My Web site may help you find out. Visit it at www.myname.com and use the Retirement Calculator. By providing your levels of savings and income and your desired retirement income, you may learn in seconds what you'll need to save over how many years to have the retirement you want. Visit my site today, or if you're not online give me a call at (714) 555-5555 and we'll do the numbers right over the phone.

Handwritten Notes
After a meeting or when you just want to send a personal hello, grab one of your personal postcards and jot a quick note. The card is professional and the client appreciates the thought.

Example
I just wanted to drop you a note to thank you for coming by the office the other day. I enjoyed seeing you and having a chance to chat. I hope we can speak soon about some specific solutions for your estate planning issues. Please call me at (714) 555-5555 if I can be of any assistance.

Four Uses For Your Personal Postcard

1. Send cards to your target markets as the key component in your "Six Week Marketing Blitz Client Generation Plan."

2. Send cards to your current clients and prospects, the key component in your "Twelve Month Drip Marketing Plan."

3. Send card to professional colleagues and referral sources to keep them aware of your activities.

4. Use cards for "thank you" notes.

Resources

- Mail It! – A highly informative resource on direct mail from Pitney Bowes that takes you through many of the ways that businesses can use direct mail to enhance business development. 247 pg., trade paperback, published by Benchmark Publications.

- Direct Marketing Techniques – Building Your Business Using Direct Mail and Direct Response Advertising, by Lois K. Geller. An informative guide to direct marketing, and a fast read. 1998, 96 pg., published by Crisp Publications.

C H A P T E R   E I G H T

Sales Letters That Work
Telling Your Best Story

A letter. It's the most basic, common piece of direct mail. It's cheap to print, easy to send out and a common presence in any mailbox. And if it's done wrong, it's the biggest waste of money in a direct mail strategy. The reasons are obvious: consumers hate junk mail, most junk mail comes in envelopes, most sales letters come in an envelope, and many look and feel like photocopied junk mail. More often than not, a consumer will tear even the most brilliantly conceived and perfectly written Sales Letter in half, and it'll hit the bottom of the trashcan without a glance.

Three Seconds is All You Have

It doesn't have to be this way. Your letter has three seconds to capture your prospect's attention; that's the amount of time they'll take to scan the headline and the first sentence, and decide if it warrants further interest. That's all the time you've got to grab them and get them reading. If you know how to do that (and you don't have to be a professional writer to do it), you can create compelling sales letters that actually get read and generate phone calls and qualified leads.

How Long Should the Letter Be?

You don't want to bore your prospect, but you don't want to come off as insubstantial, either. A strong consumer Sales Letter should be no more than four pages (two sheets of paper, printed on both sides) of tightly crafted, compelling information that offers clear benefits, a candid summary of who you are and what you do, a strong story to illustrate the power of what you're selling, and a killer call to action. Two-pagers can work, as can one-pagers...if you're writing to someone who already knows you. Your first contact with a new prospect shouldn't be made with a one-page letter.

Glossary

Unique Selling Proposition (USP): A statement that tells your prospect why what you have to offer is of value. Ideally, your USP is something fairly unique to you: your education, your identification with a certain target audience, or your leading-edge Web resources. State your USP clearly in all your marketing materials.

First, Some Sales Letter Rules...

We'll begin with some basic rules for writing effective sales letters:

- Write like you talk. The biggest mistake non-professional writers make is thinking that to talk about a serious subject like investing, you must write in some sort of stilted, stiff business-speak. Nothing could be further from the truth. These are people you're trying to reach, not MBA text books. Don't write like you're trying to sound erudite or business-like; write like you speak, like you're talking to a person sitting across a table from you. It's called writing with your own "voice."

- Speak to the individual. Some letter writers make the mistake of talking to "investors" or "consumers" instead of "you." Always talk on a one-to-one basis with your reader, using the "I have something to tell you" approach. Never generalize or lump the reader into a larger group. It kills intimacy.

- Tell a story. There's a misconception that people don't read long text, and that short bursts of copy are the only way to communicate with readers. That's simply not true. In study after study, long copy has been proven to dramatically out perform short copy. The key is to write long copy that captures people's interest by telling a compelling story. Have a beginning, middle and end, and develop your story gradually.

- Don't play your ace-in-the-hole too early. Never start right into your sales pitch at the beginning of the letter, unless you're writing a one-pager. Remember, people have a huge supply of natural sales resistance, and going full-bore into your pitch will immediately turn most of them off. Instead, foreshadow your message with a strong opening that vividly shows the reader why what you're offering is important. Then weave the pitch into the last half of the copy.

- Be direct. Don't beat around the bush. You'll only waste the reader's time. When you get to your pitch, be clear and exact about what you're selling. Remember, you're not fooling anyone with your letter; the consumer knows you're trying to sell him something. So rather than being cute and concealing your intent, write a letter that has a confident, "I'm trying to sell you this, and this is why it's so valuable to you" tone.

The Components of a Great Sales Letter

A good Sales Letter doesn't appear to have any structure behind it. It just flows, one section into the next, and pulls the reader along for the ride. But behind that appearance is a definite structure, a set of components that you'll find in virtually every Sales Letter that gets results. In developing your sales letters, you'll need to hone your skills in creating each one of these components, and be aware of how they fit into the whole letter. Each is critical to its success.

Eight Components of an Effective Sales Letter

1. The headline. If your opening is boring, nothing else matters. You must capture your reader's attention instantly with a powerful headline that has a gut-level appeal to humor, fear or some other powerful emotion. A salesy headline like "PLAN FOR YOUR RETIREMENT NOW BY INVESTING IN MUTUAL FUNDS!" is the kiss of death for your letter. But an intriguing headline like "When you're 70, will you be living off your kids?" demands that the reader think about the answer.

2. The opening sentence. There's a famous ad by advertising pioneer David Ogilvy which starts out, "They laughed when I sat down at the piano." It's famous because regardless of whether you're interested in buying the product (in this case, piano training) you're interested in finding out why people were laughing at the poor schlep tinkling the ivories. Your first sentence should grab the reader and never let go.

3. Subheads. Subheads are the smaller headlines within the body of the letter that preview sections of upcoming information. They are necessities – they break up the copy and tell the reader where to scan for certain information. Use them liberally. Nothing bores a reader like unbroken text. And remember, at most, you can only count on your prospect reading the letter's headline, first sentence, and subheads. So make your subheads count and tell the story with them in shorthand. For example, a subhead for a paragraph about saving early for retirement might read: Why You Should Open an IRA at Age 20.

4. Stories or testimonials. People love true stories, and they love quotes that come right from the horse's mouth. If you can get testimonials from current clients, or a great anecdote from a friend or client, use them! They're gold.

5. The pitch. Ask for the business! That seems elementary, but you'd be shocked at how many advisors send out letters without ever asking for business. The Sales Letter is the place to do it. The reader's not stupid; he knows you're selling financial services. So make your pitch and ask for a phone call, a meeting or a referral. Give readers a number they can call or a Web site they can visit. Otherwise, you'll never get the business.

6. The benefits. Your reader must perceive you as someone who can help him. He doesn't want to think about your reward, only his. State the benefits you offer your prospect (this is known as the Unique Selling Proposition – see Glossary above) clearly and concisely throughout the last half of your letter, and close with a concrete offer, such as a

free special report, a complimentary financial analysis, or something else of value.

7. Postscripts. A great place to really drive home any offers or special opportunities is by adding a "P.S." below your sign-off. Such items as "P.S.: The bond market is expected to take a downturn after the first of the year. Give me a call today and I'll show you how to take advantage in my "Bond Gold Seminar!" It might seem elementary, but IT WORKS.

8. Offers. If you work for a larger financial firm, you may be limited in what you can offer your prospects in terms of discounts or special promotions. But if possible, try to mix in some kind of savings to get the prospect in your office. Including a gift certificate for "$100 Off Your 1998 Personal Investment Strategy" might seem hokey, but such moves have been proven to increase response to direct mail as much as 500%.

Case Study: Direct Mail Success

Millennium Advertising has a client in Ann Arbor, Michigan who uses Sales Letters like a genius. She won't let us reveal her name, because she doesn't want competitors getting her letters, but she'll let us tell her story. We'll call her "Maggie." Maggie's direct mail campaign consists entirely of Sales Letters, sent once every two weeks to her target audience of prospects, and sent once a month to her current clients.

Does that seem to defy our advice? It does, but it just goes to show you how you can break the rules with a great idea. The secret to Maggie's success is this: all her letters are built around hysterically funny anecdotes. Some have nothing to do with money at all; they're just a riot to read. Maggie has quite an extended family, and between her family and friends, she was able to pull together about 75 great stories for her letters. She writes the letters around a specific story, then comes in at the end with an invitation to call and "hear my latest story." There's very little financial pitch, but calls pour in. People love the folksy feeling of the stories, and some local newspapers have even reprinted a few of the tales.

Maggie figures she's got enough anecdotes to last about 18 months at her current mailing rate. And the stories are doing their job: since beginning the "storytelling" campaign, her assets under management have jumped more than 130%.

Using Your Sales Letters

Writing compelling letters is only half the battle. Now you've got to deploy them effectively. Keep in mind that Sales Letters will not be the backbone of your Personal Marketing direct mail campaign; that's what your Personal Postcards are for. Sales Letters are for special needs – introducing yourself to new target audiences, doing a year-end wrap up to your current client base, informing prospects about a great offer or opportunity, and so on. Follow these guidelines for using your Sales Letters effectively:

1. Mail them once per quarter. A well-written Sales Letter is a great way to maintain a personal style of contact with your client base and your group of prospects. Every three months, as part of your regular Personal Postcard direct mail campaign, we recommend sending a two-page letter to both groups. The letter to your client base can talk about the events of the last three months, what you foresee in financial markets in the next quarter, opportunities that

might be coming up, and so on. The prospect letter can address new offers you're making or potential pitfalls they need to avoid.

2. If you decide to do a Sales Letter campaign, mail one letter per month. As with all direct mail, repetition is key. Even the "Hamlet" of all Sales Letters won't do a thing for you if you send it only once. In conducting a Sales Letter campaign, start with a longer introductory letter, continuing with a series of shorter pieces that reiterate the high points of the first letter. Then perhaps follow that with two or more one-page letters which remind readers of the content of past letters. We do recommend that if you conduct a letter campaign as opposed to a Personal Postcard campaign, you continue it for no more than six months before breaking it up with other mailers.

3. Make your letters easy to read. Print them double spaced on white or cream paper, in a font like Times Roman, Palatino or Garamond. These are fonts which are proven to be easy to read by older people.

4. Cross-promote your other marketing efforts in your letters. Mention your Personal Brochure and ask readers to call and request a copy. Give them your Web site address and invite them to visit for the latest information on your services. If you're conducting a seminar or appearing in a newspaper article, promote it.

5. Get a high-resolution digital scan of your signature. Signing 500 sales letters every month is a waste of your time. A quality scan of your John Hancock can be printed

on your letters in blue ink to look just as personal as if you'd signed it yourself.

6. Always send a business card with your letter. Since it takes multiple exposures to any marketing message for people to take action, readers may throw away your letter and card 4-5 times before they are ready to respond. When they are ready, you want them to have a business card readily available.

The Best Way to Learn

Sales letters are the easiest marketing materials to collect and copy. After all, they come to your house and office every day! We recommend that you watch your mail and instead of throwing out the many Sales Letters you receive with credit card offers and fundraising solicitations, you keep them. Read them and see what makes them effective or ineffective. Look at the effective ones and ask yourself:

Is it clear what the letter is selling?
Is it clear what I'll get for buying or calling?
Is it easy to find contact information such as a phone number?
Can I scan the headline and subheads and still get the message?

Take the best of the letters you find and follow their lesson in your own Sales Letters. There's nothing wrong with emulating what works.

Resources

1. Direct Mail Copy That Sells, by Herschell Gordon Lewis. One of the classics of direct marketing writing, this book was published back in 1984, but it's still one of the greatest guides available to writing compelling, can't-put-it-down direct mail copy. 258 pg. in paperback, published by Prentice Hall.

C H A P T E R   N I N E

Using Direct Mail Like A Pro
Getting Profitable Results

Make a Killer Impression on the Way to the Trash

Don't expect your prospects or clients to start a collection of your direct mail pieces as a hobby, no matter how good they are. Direct mail is never kept. All direct mail pieces, no matter how brilliant, have one destination: the wastebasket. The key lies in the impression it makes on the way to the trash. Also, you can't expect your direct mail to get any response two weeks after it drops. As we've stated before, all direct mail takes time and repetition.

But don't be discouraged. Used right, direct mail is your best weapon in your battle to dominate your target market. In this chapter, we're going to show you how to correctly use it.

Glossary

Direct Marketing: Any form of marketing that sells directly to the customer rather than simply placing a message where it can be seen and hoping the customer takes action. Direct mail, infomercials and telemarketing are examples of direct marketing. Most advertising in magazines and on billboards is not.

Two Main Uses for Direct Mail

So far, we've shown you two primary direct mail pieces: Personal Postcards and Sales Letters. These two mailers – as well as all other pieces of direct mail – have two main functions: to help you keep your current clients, and to help you attract qualified prospects who will become new clients.

Use #1: Keeping Current Clients

What's the number one reason that clients leave their financial advisor? It's not because of bad returns on investments, but because they feel neglected. Most consumers feel down deep that once a company or an individual gets them to sign on the dotted line, they are no longer important. That feeling is your worst enemy for client retention, and it's why you need to pay some regular attention to your existing client base.

We're not suggesting that you call each of your clients every month. That's impractical and unnecessary. Instead, mail one direct mail piece, either a Personal Postcard or a Sales Letter, every month on a set schedule to every client you want to keep (if you don't do this, you don't deserve to keep them). This kind of constant touch is the antidote for all the other financial services marketing your clients are receiving from your competitors (remember them?).

Basically, we recommend that you put all your clients on the "Twelve Month Drip Marketing Plan" to follow.

Twelve Month "Drip Marketing" Plan

Your current clients are your best source for both increasing your assets under management, your income, and your number of productive referrals. Fight the feelings of neglect and negate the effects of competitors' marketing by integrating all your clients in the Twelve Month "Drip Marketing" Plan. It will keep them informed, show them that you value open communication, and transform them into your field sales force.

This plan "drips" marketing messages to your prospects and current clients regularly and consistently. It sustains your presence in the market, stimulates referrals, and gradually erodes the resistance of reluctant prospects. Under this plan, send marketing materials once every month, rotating Personal Postcards, Personal Brochures, and Sales Letters bearing a variety of marketing, holiday and news messages.

Be sure to designate a specific date each month that your mailings will go out. This helps create a system which can run in your absence, and can help create a sense of anticipation in your recipients.

The Plan:
- Month 1:   Personal Brochure with cover letter
- Month 2:   Personal Postcard
- Month 3:   Sales letter
- Month 4:   Personal Postcard
- Month 5:   Personal Postcard
- Month 6:   Personal Brochure with cover letter asking for referrals
- Month 7:   Personal Postcard
- Month 8:   Sales letter
- Month 9:   Personal Postcard
- Month 10: Personal Postcard
- Month 11: Sales letter
- Month 12: Personal Postcard with holiday message

Use #2: Mailing to Attract New Clients

This is the widest use for direct mail: to contact people who aren't yet your customers, convince them that you offer something of value, and get them to contact you and (hopefully) become clients. When you combine a strong direct mail campaign, executed on a regular schedule, with an appropriate target audience, you have the potential for substantial, consistent gains in both client base and income.

Use "Warm Calling" to Increase Your Success

If you use direct mail and other prospecting methods in place of personal contact, you're damaging your ability to gain new clients. Direct mail, phone calls and other methods are valuable enhancements, but there is no substitute for personal contact, networking and relationship building.

When it comes to gaining new clients, direct mail alone probably isn't enough. That's why we recommend consistent follow-up with "warm calls." Unlike traditional cold calls, these calls come after several direct mailings have gone out. People are at least familiar with your name and face, and will generally be much more responsive to your message.

A perfect example is a Millennium Advertising client in San Francisco. A fee-based financial planner, she combined her direct mailings with a free, intimate seminar she was planning. After four mailings had gone out, she called the recipients and invited them to this small-scale seminar to meet her and talk frankly about what they didn't like about financial planners. More than 30 prospects attended this "bitch session" and had a ball. Eight of them became clients within the next two weeks, and four more within the next month. That's the power of "warm calling."

The Six Week "Marketing Blitz" to Attract New Clients

A Six Week Marketing Blitz Client Generation Plan is used to attract new clients to your practice. It's not a substitute for your Twelve Month Drip Marketing Plan, but the second part of a complete two-part direct mail strategy.

The plan works like this: each week for six weeks send a mailing to every prospect in your chosen target audience. As a general rule, place 150-350 potential clients on this list, or as many people as you can call to follow up. Each mailer should feature a different message about your services, but each successive mailer should build on the previous message, and all of them must include a call to action.

Since you don't want to repeat mailings to prospects who have not responded to your mailings, you may want to divide up a single target audience. For example, if your chosen target group has 1,000 households, divide them into four groups of 250 and do a six-week campaign to each, one after the other. We advise against running simultaneous campaigns, because the phone follow-up is just too time consuming.

The Plan

As with the "Twelve Month Drip Marketing Plan", make sure you have a set day of the week for mailing out each marketing piece.

- Week 1: Personal Brochure with cover letter
- Week 2: Personal Postcard
- Week 3: Sales letter
- Week 4: Personal Postcard
- Week 5: Personal Postcard
- Week 6: Sales letter followed by phone call

Divide Your Prospects Into Groups

As your "Six Week Marketing Blitz" progresses, categorize your prospects into three groups:

1. Hot prospects. These people have called you in response to your mailings. Send them a Personal Brochure immediately after the contact, then follow up with a call of your own. Put them on a "call" list and continue pursuing the appointment. Take them off your Blitz mailing list and put them on your "12 Month Drip Marketing Plan."

2. Possibles. These people have called you in response to a card, but come across like lookie-loos or disappear once you send them a brochure. Some will become Hot Prospects, while others might vanish. Regardless, you should put them on your "12 Month Drip Marketing Plan," and place any who respond to future mailings on your Hot Prospect "Call" list. After three months of your "12 Month Drip Marketing Plan," Possibles who don't respond go on your "Impossibles" list.

3. Impossibles. These people do not respond to your mailings. Do not waste your time calling them or sending brochures, and if they want off your mailing list, DO SO IMMEDIATELY. If you choose to send periodic mailings to this group, mail no more than once per quarter.

At the end of your six week campaign, you should have a list of Hot Prospects and Possibles who will receive phone calls and mailings as appropriate. You should also have new clients. Upon completing one six week plan, immediately commence a new one with a new group of prospects.

Mailing Lists

Mailing lists provide fuel for your marketing engine. Update them continually, ensuring that names and addresses are correct; enter new contacts without delay. Make sure both lists are data-archived, and keep the storage devices in a safe location.

Your mailing lists should be divided into three categories:

- Clients – Your current client base, along with all their contact information and potential referrals.

- Prospects – Everyone who's not a client in your target audience, personal contacts you've made through networking or other methods, and referrals from current clients. They all go in this database. This is the heart of your business development.

- Value Contacts – These are colleagues, professional contacts, newspaper editors, heads of professional associations – any one who may prove helpful to you in building your business.

Buying Mailing Lists vs. Building Them

We come down on one side of this issue very strongly: buy your mailing lists. Yes, you can save money by using local telephone directories or other resources to build your mailing lists. But who has the time? It's much faster and easier (and the quality of the data is higher) to purchase your mailing lists from one of several reputable mailing list companies. You'll get a complete list ready for your database application, and you'll probably get a reduced price on updates or bundled purchases. See the Resources section at the end of this chapter.

Database Software

Your mailing list will often be only as good as your database application. Invest in a quality program, such as Goldmine, Act, TeleMagic or LifeGoals. Learn how to use them properly (that means reading the manual!), and make sure you're on the software company's list to receive upgrades and new versions.

Direct Mail Fulfillment Houses

Just as you don't need to build your own mailing lists, you don't need to handle your own mailings. That's what fulfillment houses are for. These business, which are often part of larger printing operations, will label, stuff and mail your direct mail pieces for you according to your schedule. The pricing varies, but when you consider that for a fee you get a reliable system that ensures that your mailings go out on time every month, whether you're in town or not, it's worth the cost.

Check your Yellow Pages for "mail fulfillment" and start a relationship with a company.

No Such Thing as a Perfect List

Approximately 20% of the population change their name, address or phone number each year, so it's rare to get a list in which more than 80% of the data is correct. ACCEPT THIS FACT. Reputable list companies will give you a credit on your next purchase if you can provide proof of the inaccurate leads. Your best chance for a clean list is to find a company which has NCOA processing (available at most mail fulfillment houses). NCOA (National Change of Address) processing accesses the US Postal Services database, and if an addressee has submitted a change of address card they will update your mailing list. The companies below are reliable, but not perfect. Research several companies to determine the best for your needs. How do they obtain their leads? How often are they updated? What percentage do they expect to be accurate? How often is the list cleaned by NCOA processing? Purchase small quantities (250-500) from a few companies and test them by mailing. Finally, you'll get what you pay for. Cheap lists are usually cheap for a good reason.

Resources

Sources of mailing lists:

- Investor Marketing – (800) 842-9952
- American List Council – (800) ALC-LIST or www.amlist.com
- TopList – (800) 347-9267 or www.toplist.com
- Advanced Mailing Services – (760) 945-3030 or www.ams1.com
- American BusinessLists, Business and Household Lists – (800) 555-5335
- Dunn & Bradstreet, Business Lists – (800) 440-3867
- Dunnhill International List Company – (800) 386-4455
- DataMagic – (800) 926-7452
- Statewide Data Services – (800) 489-3283
- Act One – (800) 228-5478
- Glen Gary Glen Ross Inc. – (949)442-7135 or www.gggr.com
- Ark Royal Investment Leads – (800) 880-0698
- W.S. Ponton – (800) 628-7806
- Direct Search of the US – (888) 452-4126 or www.dsus.net
- Whitehall Marketing Group – (888) 241-5323
- Global Direct – (561) 586-8336

Contact Management Software:

- Act! – (800) 441-7234 or
  www.symantec.com/act01.html/index.html
- TeleMagic – (800) 835-6244 www.telemagic.com
- LifeGoals – (888) 326-0006 or www.lifegoals.com
- Goldmine – (800) 728-5783 or
  http://www.goldminesoftware.com
- Microsoft Outlook – www.microsoft.com

Identity Development
Logos, Slogans and Names

Your position is "who" you are in the minds of your clients. Personal Branding is the process of defining how you appear, time after time, to your clients and prospects. Your personal brand is the creative reflection of your position, and it manifests as your Personal or Branch Logo.

Glossary
Branding: The act of using repeated and varied marketing methods to create a level of instant identification and trust in your target audience. Branding has less to do with quality than with widespread public awareness and trust; some of the world's most recognized brands, like McDonald's, do not represent the highest quality products.

The Three Parts of Your Logo
Your Logo is a combination of your name, slogan and icon, tied together into a single unit which is used on EVERYTHING you do: business cards, brochures, direct mail, print advertising, your Web site, everything. Your Personal Logo is a graphic

representation of your position, and should be designed to appeal to your target market. It's your professional coat of arms and the symbol of your Personal Brand.

To create an effective, evocative logo which is recognizable in seconds, yet communicates a great deal about who you are and what you stand for, you must develop the three logo components with great care.

Component #1: Branch Name

As an independent financial professional, you'll most likely have a branch office of your own. Among the many decisions you face as an independent is: "What do I name my branch?" Fact is, the answer is simple, but most advisors, not knowing what to do, fall back on one of two poor choices: using their broker-dealer's name, or coming up with a deadly dull name like Retirement Planning Resources.

There is an alternative. You have four courses of action, depending on your situation:

Situation 1: If you are an independent practitioner, working alone under an independent broker-dealer—use your name. Let's take a step back. What is your doctor's name? What is the name of his practice? If he has partners, the practice may have a different name from the doctor, but if he's on his own his practice bears his name, doesn't it? That's almost always the case. In any case, even if the practice has a separate name, which name do you remember? Your doctor's. That's because you have a personal relationship.

You want your clients to have a personal relationship with you, so you should be branding your name as the name of your branch. Brand your name. Look what it's done for Charles Schwab.

Situation 2: If you are an independent practitioner working jointly with another independent, your marketing is combined and you plan to work together for at least three years-develop a team name. If you and your partner jointly market to the same clients and share marketing costs and responsibilities, you should use your last or first and last names in your branch name. So a name like "Jacobs & Martin" would be ideal.

One warning: if you are not confident that you'll be with your partner for at least three years, investing in joint marketing is probably not worth the trouble. And one other thing to consider: if a client could not come to either you or your partner and receive the same level of service, you may want to maintain separate names.

Situation 3: If you are an independent practitioner working alone under an independent broker-dealer, but you plan to hire more advisors and may have a name independent of your broker-dealer-you have two options:

Option #1: Develop a name which uses your personal name with an "and Company" attachment. We recommend that whenever possible, use your name when naming a branch. Nine of ten names chosen by advisors are generic, boring and offer no differentiation with those of competing advisors. So whenever possible use your name (first and last) combined with any of the following:

& Company
& Associates
Advisors
Partners

With this solution, a branch might be named "Scott Baldwin Partners."

Option #2: Create a branch "company" name. You may not wish to use your own name with the attachment. In that case, create a memorable corporate name for your branch. Ideally, it should appeal to your strongest target audience. So if you're selling to boat owners, a name like "Mariner Financial Advisory" might do well.

Situation 4: If you're a registered representative working for a wirehouse or independent firm which mandates that you use their name (i.e. American Express, Edward Jones, etc.) – use the corporate name. Your firm has spent millions of dollars branding their name in the minds of consumers, and your association with that name can lend immediate credibility and trust. Use the corporate name for your branch and position yourself as an advisor working under that name.

Case Study: Harry Pappas

Harry Pappas is a financial advisor with Solomon SmithBarney in Jacksonville, FL, and he's come up with a marvelous way to spread awareness of his brand identity and become known as the "broker of record" in Jacksonville. He organizes a tennis tournament.

The tournament began in 1998, when Pappas decided he wanted a way to give something back to the community in a way that would spread awareness of his name and his business. Given the 18 highly competitive tennis clubs in the Jacksonville area, a tennis tourney was a logical answer. He chose the

Ronald McDonald House as his charity, invited all 18 clubs to compete against one another for a championship cup, and paid $8,000 to cover all the costs of the first-year event. It was a (pardon the expression!) smash.

"I wanted to create something the city didn't have," he says. "People thought I was nuts, but that's when publicity happens, when people think you're crazy." The event received tremendous publicity, and Pappas intends to have it sponsored by local businesses in 1999, bringing his costs to zero. He envisions a thriving tournament which in four years will garner major corporate sponsorship and bring in $50,000 a year for Ronald McDonald House...and enhance his community image beyond measure.

"You've got to begin with the end in mind, which is one of the Seven Habits," Pappas says. "This is so easy to do. You just have to think long-term and not expect immediate results. But the results will come."

Don't Change Names on a Whim

If you have been using a branch name for a year, it has almost certainly built up "mental equity" in the minds of your target market. DO NOT CHANGE YOUR BRANCH NAME unless you are forced to, such as with legal action. Doing so can put you back to Square One in the battle for client recognition. In most circumstances, your client's allegiance is to you, not your company, so drop your broker-dealer name as soon as possible.

Component #2: Slogans

A slogan is a two-second statement that tells the reader what you stand for, what you do, and who you are. That's a tall order for 5-8 words, but it can be done. And done well, your slogan will become the most memorable part of all your Personal Marketing.

Slogans for financial advisors follow a completely different set of rules as from the rest of the advertising world. Big corporations can spend years and multi-million dollar advertising budgets to build "brand awareness" through TV, radio, and print advertising campaigns. You don't have that luxury. Major companies can create slogans that are intuitive, that reflect how they want their customers to feel about their products. Some great examples:

Nike	Just Do It.
Microsoft	Where do you want to go today?
McDonald's	Did somebody say McDonald's?
Coca-Cola	Always Coca-Cola
Marlboro	No Bull.
Apple	Think Different.

Your Slogan Must Be More Direct

As much as we love these slogans and this strategy, such emotion-based slogans are not for most advisors. You simply don't have the time or budget to create an oblique slogan that consumers have to "figure out." Utilitarian industries, such as overnight shipping, provide great examples of direct slogans:

UPS	We run the tightest ship in the shipping business.
FedEx	When it absolutely, positively has to be there overnight.

Of course, these companies no longer use these great slogans, which was a mistake on their part. But you get the point. Anyway, we've broken down the three best financial advisor slogan approaches:

Approach #1: Tell people what you do and for whom you do it.

Examples:
- Financial Planning for St. Louis Professionals
- South Florida Estate Planning
- The Doctor's Financial Planner
- Financial Advisory Services for Women

Approach #2: Tell people what you do and the benefit of your service.

Examples:
- Financial Planning for Peace of Mind
- On Course Estate Planning
- The Conservative Choice for Tax-free Income
- Investment Planning for Family Goals
- Succession Planning for Families in Business

Approach #3: Break the rules.
If you are using a company name which already says what you do, you may use a traditional advertising slogan which is a creative expression of your unique benefit. That doesn't mean to emulate Nike; your slogan should still relate to smart financial services.

Examples:
- For Success, Do the Right Things Right
- Sowing the Seeds of Prosperity
- Taking Professionals to the Summit of Success
- Making Technology Your Best Investment Ally

Try to keep you slogan to 4-6 words if possible; go to 10 words if you have to. You may break grammar rules; Apple did it beautifully with "Think Different." And don't put your slogan in quotations. It is a rookie maneuver.

Component #3: Logo Icons

Icons are the graphics that go along with your name and slogan in your logo. Some logos will not have any graphics other than your name; however, we recommend that you have a designer develop some sort of graphic element to accompany your name. It makes your logo more memorable, and can tie in more directly to your Personal Marketing position. For instance, if you've chosen to market to pilots because of your aviation background, a jet graphic in your logo is perfect.

First, we're going to stop you from making a mistake often made by real estate agents. When Realtors (who are generally very adept at Personal Marketing) create logos, they often use either their headshot or a graphic of a house as their icon. Don't make the same mistake. Photos do not reproduce well in logos, and make you look like an amateur.

As for houses, they are 100% cliche. Financial advisors make the same mistake when they use one of these overused icons: columns, currency, Wall Street, eagles, lighthouses, compasses, and chart graphics. Choose an icon which reflects your target market or what you do.

All Colors Are Not Created Equal

There's one more matter to consider in creating your logo: color. There are five main colors: red, orange, yellow, green and blue. You may also consider three neutral colors: black, white and gray. In creating your logo, stick to one of the main colors rather than an intermediate or mixed color. But which color?

Colors on the red end of the spectrum are focused slightly behind the retina of the eye and appear to move towards the eye. Colors on the blue end of the spectrum are focused slightly in front of the retina and therefore appear to move away from you. For those reasons, red is the color of energy, excitement and attention. Blue is the opposite: peaceful, tranquil and laid back. In the world of marketing, red attracts attention, blue communicates stability. Coca-Cola is red. IBM is blue. No coincidence there.

Over the years some colors have become identified with various attributes, occasions and movements:

- White – purity, as in a white wedding
- Black – luxury, as in a tuxedo or a black Mercedes
- Yellow – caution, as in a yellow light, sign or flag
- Blue – leadership, such as in a blue ribbon awarded to a winner
- Purple – royalty, as in the well-known bag used by Crown Royal scotch
- Green – nature and health, as in Greenpeace and Healthy Choice foods
- Red – attention, used in many consumer brands such as such as Texaco, Marlboro and McDonald's.

When selecting a color for your logo, ask yourself about the mood you want to establish. In most circumstances, logos should contain two colors. Using four colors is expensive and often clutters a logo. The best logos are generally one of the five main colors and a neutral, usually black.

Pulling it All Together

Once you have your name, your slogan and your icon, you can pull them all together to create your logo. They should all appear as a single unit, available to be placed on all your materials. By NASD regulations, your broker-dealer information must also be on all your marketing materials, but depending on the name recognition or your broker-dealer you may choose to place their logo on your materials as well. If you work for a well-known broker-dealer, you may decide to run their logo as large as yours. Some broker-dealers may require it. Handle the situation as the need arises.

Examples of Personal Logo, a Team Logo and a Company Logo. All incorporate slogans of various kinds. One note: if your logo makes it clear what you do, your slogan can be less direct.

A Word About Designers...

This is the only area of Personal Marketing where we'll recommend that you seek professional assistance. Logo design is an intricate, demanding art, and you would be wise to seek the help of a professional designer. They can choose the proper typeface for your name, place your slogan in the proper area, and create an icon that suits your personal style. For an average fee of $1,500 to $2,500, it's money well spent to have a great Logo.

Resources

- The Non-Designer's Design Book – Design and Typographic Principles for the Visual Novice, by Robin Williams and Carol Quandt (editor). An outstanding primer on design principles for people with little or no design background. 1997, 144 pg., published by Peachpit Press.

- Graphis World Trademarks – Logo Compendium, edited by Rick Eiber. It's a costly ($175) book, but this collection of killer logos is an invaluable resource if you really want to learn what makes a great logo last before designing your own. 1997, Graphis Press.

Web Sites
Why You Must Be Online

You must have a Web site by January 1st, 2002. Period. Unless you've been living in a cave in West Virginia, you know the Internet and the World Wide Web are the most powerful tools for personal and business communication that have ever been devised. And as you have also seen, they are fast revolutionizing the world of finance.

Today, consumers can trade stocks online at dozens of Web sites. They can get 15-minute delayed stock quotes all over the Web, and locate financial advisors via a variety of search engines. As more consumers get online and use the Web as their main financial resource, it becomes even more critical that financial professionals develop and maintain a presence on the Web. Basically, if you don't have a Web site, you won't be in business very long.

See the Glossary of Basic Web Terms at the end of the chapter for some essential Web lingo.

Six Ways the Web Can Help You Grow Your Business

1. Provide a 24/7 source of information for your prospects and clients. A good Web site is a completely non-confrontational way for prospects to find out about you without worrying that they're going to be subject to a sales pitch.

2. Provide a way for your clients to access their investment accounts online, without your intervention. Empowerment and freedom of information are hallmarks of the Web, and the more power and knowledge you can put into your clients' hands, the happier they'll be.

3. Fast communication. Clients can communicate with you via e-mail no matter where you or they are, enabling you to respond quickly to concerns or questions.

4. Serve as a platform for value-added services. Some advisors have turned their sites into hubs for financial research and investment journals. Others provide a wide range of calculators and other functions, allowing clients to figure retirement savings and so on. Turning your Web site into a valuable resource turns you into one as well.

5. Helps build your database. Through such simple features as allowing people to sign up for an e-mail newsletter, you can capture user information on your site and build your database of contacts and prospects without making a single call.

6. Positions you as a technically savvy financial professional. In this industry, there will soon be two kinds of advisors: the tech-smart and the dinosaur. Guess who the tech-savvy

investor is going to want to work with? A Web site will extend your brand into cyberspace.

People Are Using the Web

The Web is becoming big business, and a fast-growing number of educated consumers are using it to make purchasing decisions. Consider the amount of money spent purchasing consumer goods on the Web:

1998: $4.8 billion
1999 (projected): $8.1 billion
2000 (projected): $14.5 billion

The Web is no longer a fringe phenomenon. It's a force in the daily lives of more than 60 million Americans, and the numbers are growing. It's time to add some geek-chic to your identity.

Don't Support Your Local Web Designer

Right off the bat, some good advice: don't hire your cousin to create your Web site. You'll need four skill sets to create your site:

- Writer – produces the copy that will appear on your site, and may also lay out the site structure.

- Graphic designer – creates the "look and feel" of the site, including the interface the user employs to navigate around the site.

- Programmer – the person who writes the computer code that makes the site function, allows links to work, and so on.

- Web marketing expert – someone who can instruct you in setting up your site to capture leads and attract prospects, and help you drive traffic to the site.

These may all be one and the same person, but more often than not you'll need up to four people with proven skills. Don't rely on a "garage shop," guys slaving away in their basement over endless Dr. Peppers, to design your site. This is your business we're talking about, not some alternative hip-hop magazine. Hire real Web professionals to create your site, and look at their existing site work before choosing them.

What's In Your Site?

There are two categories of content that you'll feature on your Web site: Personal Marketing Content and Feature Content. Personal Marketing Content represents the essentials of your site; without it, you may as well not have a site at all. Feature Content represents value-added services you're providing for your clients on your site. Having Feature Content is optional, but it can add great value and "stickiness" (the ability of your site to bring people back to it and keep them there) to your Web site.

Personal Marketing Content

There are five basic areas of Personal Marketing Content, each with its own Web page within your site:
1. Home page
2. Personal information
3. Product/service information
4. Company information
5. Request information

Home Page – The first page people see when they come to your site. This is your prime real estate, where you have to convince people to stay. Tell them who you are and what you do, and make sure any special features of your site are promoted very aggressively on the home page. MAKE SURE your home page has a very obvious e-mail link users can click on to send an instant e-mail to you.

Personal Information – This is the page that reflects your Personal Brochure content. You may want to reproduce much of the text from your brochure on this page, since it makes the statements about you that you want.

Product/Service Information – Here is where you'll describe in detail the kinds of products and services you offer. Keep it brief, but make sure the consumer knows the kind of work you do and how you can help him.

Company Information – This is where to mention your broker-dealer. If you work with a well-known company, be generous with the information; if not, just provide enough info to reassure the user that your broker-dealer is experienced and reputable.

Request Information – This is basically a page with an online form where users can fill in questions and their contact information and e-mail you. You can call them, send a Personal Brochure, e-mail them in reply or take whatever action is appropriate.

Feature Content
This is where things get good. With the continuous advance of Web technology, there's an almost limitless universe of things you can put on your site which will offer information,

communication or added value to your clients and prospects. Most are database driven and will cost substantially more to develop than a simple Personal Marketing site, but they have great payoffs.

You should explore the Web yourself to learn about all the options, but we've boiled them down to a manageable Top 13 User-Friendly Web Features, and categorized them by how they benefit the client, and how they benefit you, the advisor.

Top 14 User-Friendly Web Features

Feature: Savings Calculator
User Benefit: Allows users to figure how their investments will grow over defined periods of time or for certain goals like college.
Advisor Benefit: Positions your site as a valuable resource.

Feature: Retirement Calculator
User Benefit: Allows users to enter their income, savings and lifestyle factors and determine how much they'll need to save to have the post-retirement income they desire.
Advisor Benefit: Positions your site as a valuable resource, positions you as a retirement specialist.

Feature: College Calculator
User Benefit: Allows users to figure out what a four-year college education will cost by the time their child is ready, and how much to save to pay for it.
Advisor Benefit: Positions you as a full-service specialist whose interested in the welfare of the entire family, not just the wage earners.

Feature: Stock Quotes
User Benefit: Lets users see 15-minute delayed NYSE, NASDAQ and AMEX quotes each time the reload your site pages; other versions allow users to enter a stock ticker symbol or company name and get the latest price for that single stock.
Advisor Benefit: Gives users a reason to come back to your site for the latest market data.

Feature: E-mail Newsletter
User Benefit: Lets users sign up for a regular newsletter with financial tips and market updates, sent to them automatically by e-mail.
Advisor Benefit: Allows you to capture user names and e-mail addresses on your site (preferably on your home page) to be used later on for direct e-mail prospecting.

Feature: Industry News
User Benefit: Lets users view breaking financial news stories directly on your site.
Advisor Benefit: Positions your site as a valuable news hub, keeps users coming back for more news.

Feature: News and Research Hub
User Benefit: Turns your site into a hub where users can find links to a variety of financial news sources and corporate research information.
Advisor Benefit: Positions your site as a valuable information resource for investors.

Feature: Client Account Access
User Benefit: Provides a password-protected area of your site where clients can access their accounts, see their returns, and look at trends.

Advisor Benefit: Gives your clients more information and control, two keys to better client relationships.

Feature: Search Engine
User Benefit: Allows users to either search your site for information or to search the entire Web for the data they seek.
Advisor Benefit: Positions your site as a valuable resource.

Feature: Document Download
User Benefit: Turns your site into a center where users can download printable versions of a variety of important documents such as tax forms.
Advisor Benefit: Positions your site as a resource that adds convenience to everyday life.

Feature: Automatic Portfolio Updates
User Benefit: Clients can choose to have e-mail automatically sent to them whenever a selected investment or group of investments takes a specified action, i.e. a company's stock drops more than 25%.
Advisor Benefit: Provides an instant way for you to keep your clients informed about their investments.

Feature: Refer a Friend
User Benefit: Allows users to enter e-mail addresses of one or more contacts, and have an automatic e-mail sent to those people informing them about something worth seeing on your site.
Advisor Benefit: Allows you to capture additional e-mail addresses and provides a 24/7 way to generate referral business.

Feature: Download Brochure

User Benefit: Allows prospects to download a printable copy of your Personal Brochure.

Advisor Benefit: Gives you a way to get your best marketing materials in the hands of prospects automatically.

Feature: Request an Appointment

User Benefit: Allows prospects to fill out a form requesting a specific appointment day and time with you, prints out a calendar showing the appointment, and sends them an e-mail reminder the day before the appointment.

Advisor Benefit: Gives you a hands-off way to set appointments and track time commitments.

Some Tips When Designing Your Site

- Forget heavy graphics. Big pictures take time to load and will just annoy your users. Keep your layout clean and easy to view. A good designer will make the most of graphic limitations to design a compelling user interface.

- Forget audio and video. The Web isn't TV, no matter what the movies show. You won't have video playback or audio on your site, at least not for a few years.

- Keep copy brief. People shouldn't have to read 1,000 words on your investment skills. The Web is a hard medium on the eyes, so keep copy succinct.

- Make sure users always know where they are. The best method is to have some sort of site map showing them where along the branching pages they are.

• Tie in to your other marketing materials. Use the same graphics from your Personal Brochure and use your logo. You can of course use new graphics, but make sure they tie in to your offline marketing in some way.

If You Build it, They Won't Come

You've got a great Web site. So what? If you think that just because you have a Web site thousands of people will flock to it, you are in dreamland. There are about three million sites competing for consumers' attention, including E-Trade and other financial juggernauts. The fact is, if you want to drive traffic to your site, you must market it online and offline.

Some of the best ways to drive traffic to your site:

• Send a Personal Postcard to your current clients. This is a match made in heaven. Each month you can send your current clients a Personal Postcard promoting a different feature of your Web site. These are people who already know you and like you; they're the perfect Web site audience.

• Send a Personal Postcard to prospects as part of your ongoing marketing. Dedicate one card to your new Web site and all its value-added features.

• Submit your site to all the major search services (Yahoo!, Excite, Alta Vista, Goto.com, etc.) to give yourself the best chance of being found during a search. Update your search engine listings as often as possible, monthly if you're doing it on your own, daily if you hire a Web promotion company that can do it automatically.

• Submit your site to the various referral services that help people find financial advisors in their area.

- Promote your site by including your Web address on all materials: your business cards, your letterhead, any outdoor or print advertising, etc.

- Promote your site at all your seminars and speaking engagements. Include the address on seminar flyers or handouts.

- Get banner exchanges with other Web sites. In these arrangements, you place a banner or link to their site on yours, and they do the same for you.

Getting a URL

A URL (Uniform Resource Locator) is your Web address, beginning with "www." Keep your URL simple. Ideally, you should use your name, as in "www.johnjacobsen.com." If you have a partnership, use both names like this: "www.powers-baker.com." To obtain a URL, log on to www.networksolutions.com.

A Glossary of Basic Web Terms:

- World Wide Web – The Internet is the entire global network of connected computers. The Web is a part of that network that presents information graphically, and in some cases with audio, video and animation.

- Download – To save a document or piece of software from the Internet to your own computer.

- Modem – The device which connects you to the Internet through a phone line or other connection.

- Browser – The software used to browse the Web, generally either Netscape Communicator or Microsoft Internet Explorer.
- E-mail – Electronic mail, the booming method of instant electronic communication.

Resources

- Creating Web Pages for Dummies – 4th Edition, by Bud E. Smith, Arthur Bebak and Kevin Werbach. The latest in this hugely successful how-to franchise, this book takes novices through every step of creating a successful Web site. 1999, 360 pages, published by IDG Books Worldwide.

- Project Cool (www.projectcool.com) – The leading Web site for both showcasing the best of Web design and for advice and information for experts and novices.

- Web Site Journal (www.websitejournal.netscape.com) – A fabulous site that focuses not only on developing a winning site, but also on keeping it fresh and effective once it's up.

Advanced Marketing Tools
PR, Advertising, and More

Once you have mastered the art and science of basic Personal Marketing, you may find yourself wanting to move onto more sophisticated marketing methods. You may do this because you find that more competitors are duplicating your Personal Marketing efforts, or simply that your results have "plateaued" and you need to use some new methods to generate new business. That's fine, but before you venture into new marketing territory, ask yourself the following:

- Do I understand Personal Marketing well enough to apply the principles to new media?

- Do I understand the new advertising methods well enough to get the best value?

- Do I have the budget to venture into new areas?

We'll leave it to you to answer those questions. In this chapter, we'll give you some basic education about four of the most common advanced marketing tools: Advertising, Broadcast, Outdoor, and Public Relations.

Advertising

When we say advertising, we mean print advertising, the kind you see every day in newspapers and magazines. Advertising is a passive medium that gives you no control over who you reach, but it does offer you a hands-off way of communicating your position and message to many thousands of people without lifting a finger.

Advertising is a tricky business. Many advisors want to create ads that shove a benefit into the reader's face, as if that will be compelling. Take the same approach to your advertising that you do with your Personal Brochure: appeal to the emotions first, the logic center second. The most important job your ad has is to stop the reader in his tracks. Without that stopping power, it has no chance of generating any phone calls.

For most advisors, we don't recommend advertising for two reasons: 1) unless you're in a small market, it's prohibitively expensive, and 2) it's very unfocused, and your message "spills over" to a lot of people who aren't in your target market. In general, only use advertising if you can run it in a highly targeted publication, such as a newspaper for a planned community, and if you have the marketing materials and budget to support your ads.

- Benefits: The ability to reach a wide audience at one time, without any involvement from the advertiser; the ability to spread your face, name, position and brand identity throughout your target area; the ability to generate a high volume of calls in a short time.

- Risks: Poorly created ads can cost you thousands of dollars and produce no leads.

- Costs: Costs will vary depending on the publication, its circulation, and whether your ad is color or black and white. Call any publications you're interested in for a media kit; this will contain the latest ad rates and instructions for insertion. Keep in mind a full-page ad in a color monthly magazine can run into the tens of thousands of dollars.

- Logistics: You'll need to design your ad and have it output by a company that creates film and paper output for printers. Talk to your printer to get more information about this process.

- Beware of poorly printed publications that offer you rock-bottom advertising rates. They may give you space for next to nothing, but if your ad looks terrible it will only hurt your image.

- Jump at the opportunity if you get a great deal on placement in a quality publication, even if the cost is a little high. It's worth it to see what kind of results your ad can generate.

Tips for doing it right

- Make sure your phone number and Web address are prominent in the ad.

- Most publications offer a discount if you buy space in more than one issue, so ask for it.

- Don't use a headshot of yourself in your ad.

- Include some kind of offer in your ad, such as a free special report or a discount on fees for the first three months of financial planning.

- Make your headline short and powerful, appealing to the emotions.

- Take a look at the best print advertising and see what makes it work.

Broadcast

For our purposes, broadcast refers to financial talk shows on local radio stations. These can be difficult to get, and you need the on-air skills and the time to make them work, but if you can get a radio program, it can do extraordinary things for your business.

Radio programs can range from brief market updates to full 30 or 60 minute call in programs where you take calls from consumers needing financial advice (getting such a show should be your ultimate goal). Doing a radio program might seem like foreign territory, but you'd be surprised how many local radio stations have airtime to fill. If you have a good voice, are comfortable speaking to others, and feel like you can answer a wide range of questions on the fly, a radio program might be an ideal vehicle for you.

A well-produced radio program lends an immediate sense of success and credibility to your business, establishing the idea that "This guy must be doing well if he's on the radio." Radio also gives you the same wide reach as print advertising.

- Benefits: Wide reach; an image of success; powerful cross-promotional ability; the ability to target a specific audience by listening habits.

- Risks: Bad radio makes you sound like an amateur.

- Costs: Minimal. If you get a show and you want to do it from your office, you'll need a remote audio console, which can cost several thousand dollars. Other than that, all costs are borne by the station. One other possible cost: many stations will expect you to invest in some advertising on the station in return for the time to do your show. Find out airtime rates before you commit.

- Logistics: You'll need to practice your on-air personality, have market updates and other critical financial information available, and be trained on using either in-studio equipment or a remote console.

- Beware of committing yourself to more time for a program than you can afford, or of getting into something that you're not comfortable with. If you dread speaking to callers, your show will die a quick death.

• Jump at the opportunity if you have a personal contact at a local station.

Tips for doing it right

• Simply contact multiple local stations and ask them if they would be interested in a financial call-in show. It's a hot topic with listeners all over the U.S.

• Get a show on a talk station, not a music or sports station.

• Be willing to start by doing brief market updates at the end of a station's financial or news programming.

• Try to get a title from the station such as Business Editor or Financial Editor.

• Always have something to promote during your show. When listeners call, suggest that for further answers to their questions, they see your Web site.

• Have a relaxed on-air personality. Don't try to sell anyone. Make any suggestions to come to a seminar or hit a Web site subtle.

• You'll have a better chance of landing a program if you use your Personal Brochure and other tools to establish credibility with a Program Director.

Case Study: Marty Schneider

Marty Schneider, a CFP with The Advisors Group in San Diego, CA, has turned a chance meeting at a health club into a thriving radio show that got his business booming. While exercising, he met the manager of KPRZ 1210 AM, a local radio station, and started talking. When the manager discovered Schneider's profession, he asked him about doing market reports during news broadcasts. Schneider agreed.

Later, those reports grew into a weekend live call-in program, and now, five years after that fateful meeting, Schneider has his own five-day-per-week, 30-minute call-in program that he conducts from his office. He purchased a broadcast system for his office at a cost of about $4,000, but the station handles everything else. An engineer screens the calls and Schneider simply wings it, dispensing financial advice on the fly.

Of course, he doesn't do this without a strategy. "I try to convert callers to come to my seminars by being a little vague about my answers," he says, "and suggesting that to get the whole picture, they should attend my seminar, which is true, by the way. I have a 90% consultation request rate from my seminars, 80% of those people actually come in, and 75% of those become clients. So I'm converting about 50% of all my seminar attendees, partially due to the radio program."

Outdoor

Billboards. Bus boards. Bus stop benches. Ads on the side of moving vehicles (such as taxis). They're all examples of outdoor advertising. It's very widely used; look at the many bus stop benches you see with Realtors' faces plastered on them. The problem is, outdoor advertising tends to be the least professional and most "hokey" of all the advanced ad methods in this chapter. It's easy to do badly, and hard to do right.

The biggest mistake most financial advisors make when they do outdoor advertising is trying to make it direct response advertising. But think about it—when a person sees an outdoor ad, he's probably whizzing by in a car or watching a bus go past. In order to make these ads generate phone calls, advisors (and other advertisers) put two things on their ads: their names, and their phone numbers, both huge. There's no art, no positioning, and no branding. Just desperation to generate calls.

We recommend the opposite. If you decide to do outdoor advertising, make it about branding first, direct response second. Get your name and face known. We've seen several effective advisor billboards that included nothing more than a very powerful photo of the advisor and his Web site address. Nothing else. It's okay to put your phone number on your bus board, but don't make it the focus.

Most important, talk to the outdoor agencies in your area and get information on traffic patterns, costs of multiple placements, and so on. Many of the companies who sell outdoor space will also help you produce your ad.

For most advisors, we don't recommend outdoor. It's an advanced tool that's primarily useful for spreading your brand identity throughout a region, not for generating phone calls. Have you ever called a number from a billboard? Almost no one does. They're just more likely to hit a Web site.

- Benefits: Gives you a tangible presence in the community, spreads your name, face and brand identity.

- Risks: Can be costly for multiple placements, and if you don't target the right locations for your target audience, you'll get few (if any) results.

- Costs: Costs vary widely, depending on the type of media (highway-side billboards are the most expensive), the location and how many ads you place within a certain region. Contact all the outdoor ad companies for specific price lists. You'll also pay for design and ad production, including color printing if required.

- Logistics: You'll need your ad written and designed, then printed by a specialty printer and placed on the various outdoor media by a team.

- Beware buying outdoor for size only. A big billboard in a bad spot won't benefit you at all, but a bus stop billboard outside a senior citizens center might jump start your retirement planning business immensely.

- Jump at the opportunity to cross-promote your outdoor with other advertising. For example, if you have an event coming up that you're promoting on radio, also buy an outdoor ad.

Tips for doing it right

- Issue a press release about your outdoor advertising. It's rare for advisors to take outdoor ads, so it's news.

- Send Personal Postcards to clients and prospects suggesting they look for your bus stop board at the corner of Fifth and Grand.

- Don't try to do too much with your outdoor ad. Remember, people are in motion when they see it. Keep it powerful and simple.

- The headline is everything. Make sure it's strong.

Public Relations (PR)

PR costs little or no money, but takes a great deal of time. Essentially, Public relations is the art of generating press coverage, primarily in print, though there are possibilities for radio and online.

The basic activity involved in PR is sending press releases to your local publications. The objective is to cultivate relationships with editors over time, eventually leading to one or more of the following outcomes:

- Coverage of your special event or seminar
- Use of you as a source for a news story or feature
- A story about you and your financial planning business
- You get offered a financial column in the publication

To begin your PR campaign, we recommend sending a press kit to the editors of your local newspapers and magazines. Do not contact them by phone; this is considered unprofessional and will probably get you labeled as just another pushy salesman. Send a press kit containing a press release about your business, your personal bio, your Personal Brochure, and a black and white photo. Top it off with a cover letter outlining your areas of financial expertise and your assertion that you would love to be of help as a source for any financial article. Always include a business card.

After the initial mailing, send a release every month to the same editorial pool. They will probably get tossed initially, but eventually editors start recognizing the same name coming across their desks every month, and will call you. It just takes time.

Press coverage is the best advertising short of personal referral. It's objective from a trusted source, it's widespread and it's comprehensive (you can say a lot more about yourself in a 350 word column than in a 1/4-page ad).

- Benefits: Instant credibility, wide reach.

- Risks: You can spend a lot of time courting editors who, for some reason, will never call you.

- Costs: Minimal. Folders to mail your press kit, the cost of 8 x 10 black and white glossy photos, and mailing costs to 6-10 editors.

- Logistics: You MUST know the standard professional press release style used everywhere. Look on the PR sections of various corporate Web sites and you'll see the standard form. Follow this form every time you send a release.

- Beware being too persistent in your contact with editors. Many are very busy and have no time to talk with you. Keep in mind that they are professionals, and if you respect their time, when they finally have time to notice you, you'll get the same respect. Conversely, an angry journalist can bury you. Ask Nixon.

- Jump at the opportunity to establish a personal relationship with an editor. If you can buy him dinner or grab a few beers, do it. Building a friendship with an editor, as long as you don't try to take too much advantage, can get you more coverage than you ever thought possible.

Tips for doing it right

- Send a release every month, even if your news is simply hiring a new assistant. Find something newsworthy. Think of it as direct mail for the press; it's about repetition.

- Keep your releases to one page, except perhaps for the first release you send with your press kit.

- Write in "inverted pyramid style": the who, what, where, when, how and why information in the first paragraph, with information of lesser importance as you go down the page.

- Keep the writing newsy and factual. Don't editorialize.

- Get custom Rolodex cards printed and send them to each editor to keep in his card file. Make yourself a story resource.

- If you have an idea for a column and you think you can produce one on a weekly or monthly basis, submit it to the appropriate editors. Keep in mind there's nothing that stops you from hiring a ghostwriter.

Resources

- Ogilvy on Advertising, by David Ogilvy. This is a classic by the man many consider to be the father of modern advertising. It's a timeless introduction to the forms, theories and approaches behind all kinds of advertising. 1983, 224 pg., published by Vintage Books.

- PR Newswire (www.prnewswire.com) – The leading public relations and news wire service on the Web, and a terrific place to learn more about how PR works.

- The Handbook of Strategic Public Relations and Integrated Communications, by Clark L. Caywood. A high-level guide for those interested in really learning the ins and outs of making PR work for them. 1997, published by McGraw-Hill.

- Advertising Without An Agency: A Comprehensive Guide to Radio, Television, Print, Direct Mail and Outdoor Advertising for Small Business, by Kathy J. Kobliski. The title says it all. 1998, 175 pg., published by Psi Research Oasis Press.

Part IV
Start Your
Marketing

Creating Your One Year Marketing Plan

Now we're down to it. You've gotten an education in the tools and theories of Personal Marketing. We'll now walk you through creating your own One Year Marketing Plan, a plan that if followed properly, should allow you to double your income and grow your business beyond your wildest expectations.

Let's get busy.

A Step-By-Step Guide to Getting Started

Tackling your own marketing plan for the first time can be nerve-wracking. That's why we've given you this step-by-step guide to what you should be doing, both at the beginning of your campaign and as the months pass. Getting through all the steps should take you from six to eight weeks, at which point you'll be ready to hit the market running.

If this seems like a lot of work, consider this: a well-executed marketing plan is your insurance policy against the negative effects of market fluctuations. If you'd like your business to be thriving while others are worrying about markets falling, your marketing plan is your key. But it only works if you follow through with it, even when it seems to be generating no results.

Step One: Set Your Goals

To set a realistic income goal, ask yourself the following questions:

- How much did I earn in the previous 12 months?

- What are my current fixed expenses?

- What new expenses will I incur as part of implementing a new marketing plan, e.g. advertising, personal brochure, personal assistant?

- What outside considerations may influence my ability to increase my income in the next twelve months, increase my existing market share, and develop a new market or new target?

- What kind of income do I want to be earning 12 months from now? 24 months? 36 months?

Break down your desired first year income goal in to quarters, and you'll get a clear idea of how much your production must increase to meet your goal.

Your goals must also include more general objectives. Ask yourself:

- How many more clients do I want to attract in 12 months?

- What net worth would I like my new clients to have?

- Do I want to be known among the general public or just among my peers?

- Do I want to attract an offer from another firm?

- What kind of lifestyle would I like to be living in a year? Three years?

Step Two: Establish a Marketing Budget

Many world-class marketers spend between 20% and 35% of their income on marketing. How much are you willing to spend to attain new, income-producing clients? Your answer will help define your marketing budget. Many top producers begin by investing up to 70% of their gross income in order to build their businesses. The smaller your income, the greater the necessity for you to spend in order to realize this growth.

Plan on spending...
- 5 to 10% of your income to maintain your current production.

- 10 to 30% of your income goal to expand your business, depending on the competitiveness of the target market you select.

- 40% of your gross income if you are launching a push into a target market where you've never marketed before. That's what it will take to build an image, create awareness and call clients to your door.

Create a month-by-month, line-item budget that covers all marketing-related expenses, including:
- Creative costs (writing, design, Web programming)
- Printing
- Photocopying
- Ad placement
- Postage
- Bulk mail permits
- Direct mail fulfillment services
- Mailing lists
- Hosting your Web site
- Phones
- Travel
- Assistant salaries
- Photography

This is also the time to determine if you'll need to hire anyone to help you implement your marketing. This could be full-time assistant or a freelance administrative assistant. Include the salary in your budget.

Step Three: Establish Your Essentials
Finalize your essential marketing elements:
- Position
- Target Audiences—choose just one for your initial marketing
- Marketing Channels—remember to find five channels you can use to reach your prospects

Step Four: Gather Your Resources

What marketing tools will you use? Chances are you're planning to use a Personal Brochure, Personal Postcard, Sales Letters and Personal Branding tools. Should you add a Web site, or perhaps a public relations campaign? Now is the time to determine what tools you'll use, how many you'll create or print, and when they will be completed.

This is also the time to locate needed resources. These may include a printer, a direct mail fulfillment house, professional organizations (Chambers of Commerce, etc.), a market research company and photographer.

At this stage, you'll also want to create your Contact List and purchase your mailing list for your target audience. The Contact List is a database of current clients, personal contacts, professional contacts and colleagues to whom you'll send your marketing materials. Verify the information for each person before mailing. Make sure both lists are stored in a quality database program and properly backed up on disk.

Step Five: Phase Your Plan

No matter how big your budget is, you won't want to enact your entire marketing plan at once. It will be too much to handle. Divide your 12-month strategy into phases, each with a specific goal, and launch a new phase as you see the previous phase taking effect. We've found that Phase One should be given 9-12 months to take effect, while subsequent phases can take from 3-6 months. The following is a very strong phased plan you should feel free to copy:

Phase One: Build Your Identify and Differentiate Yourself

- Begin sending your "Six Week Blitz Marketing Client Generation Plan" to your target audience and your "Twelve Month Drip Marketing Plan" to your existing client base.

- If you have a Personal Brochure, Personal Postcard and Personal Logo, distribute your brochure to your Contact List. Mail two copies of the brochure to every client and colleague on your Contact List, along with a cover letter asking for referrals.

- Distribute your new identity materials (business cards, brochures) in any way possible.

- Develop a system for tracking the results of your direct mail.

- Launch your Web site.

Phase Two: Capitalize On New Business and Greater Visibility

- Take advantage of new clients attracted by Phase One to ask them for referrals.

- Launch a more sophisticated direct mail campaign, such as one using only Sales Letters, to desirable but reluctant prospects.

- Attend networking meetings.

- Seek public speaking or panel opportunities.

- Take out print ads in local publications.

Phase Three: Seize Increased Market Share

- Issue a monthly e-mail newsletter.

- Purchase outdoor advertising in target communities.

- Conduct research and identify new target markets.

- Add features to your Web site such as retirement calculators or message boards.

- Develop and mail a new Personal Postcard campaign.

- Continue your client maintenance and referral programs.

Phase Four: Reinvest Your Increased Earnings

- Begin hosting a financial call-in program on a local radio station or cable access channel.

- Sponsor a local event.

- Hold your own large public seminar.

- Adjust Personal Postcard campaigns based on tracking and begin "Six-Week Blitz Marketing Client Generation Plan" campaign again with new target markets.

Phase Five: Evaluate Your Results

- Check income goals against actual performance.

- Track all direct mail responses for effectiveness and discard ineffective messages or media.

- See how well you have kept to your schedule.

- Establish new goals for the next 12 months.

- Create a new budget.

During all your marketing phases, your "Twelve Month Drip Marketing Plan" should always be running, always to a wider and wider audience.

Step Six: Create Your Action Plan

After defining your target and marketing tools, design a 12-month action plan. Create date-triggered procedures in your office which will automatically execute your marketing plan as you focus on your day-to-day servicing and business activities. Your marketing plan should run even when you're out of town, on business or across the country on vacation.

Compile all this information into a binder and use it as your Personal Marketing Bible. Post your Action Plan in a large format on your wall or somewhere you can see it and refer to it easily. It will be your guide as you step into the world of Personal Marketing...and make a lot more money!

Resources

- The Marketing Plan: How to Prepare and Implement It, by William M. Luther. A comprehensive guide to creating and using your most important strategic tool. 1992, 209 pg., published by the American Management Assn.

- Center for Business Planning (www.businessplans.org/business.html) – An excellent online center for researching and writing business and marketing plans, getting online assistance, and more.

Marketing Plan Worksheet

	Activity	January	February	March	April	May	June
Client Generation	Date						
	Personal Brochure						
	Sales Letter						
	Postcard						
Client Maintenance	Activity						
	Date						
	Personal Brochure						
	Sales Letter						
	Postcard						
Advertising	Activity						
	Date						
	Personal Brochure						
	Sales Letter						
	Postcard						
Internet	Activity						
	Date						
	Personal Brochure						
	Sales Letter						
	Postcard						
Public Relations	Activity						
	Public Relations						
	Update Press Kit						
	Contact Editor						
	Press Release						
	Public Speaking						

Marketing Plan Worksheet

	Activity	July	August	September	October	November	December
Client Generation	Date						
	Personal Brochure						
	Sales Letter						
	Postcard						
	Activity						
Client Maintenance	Date						
	Personal Brochure						
	Sales Letter						
	Postcard						
	Activity						
Advertising	Date						
	Personal Brochure						
	Sales Letter						
	Postcard						
	Activity						
Internet	Date						
	Personal Brochure						
	Sales Letter						
	Postcard						
	Activity						
Public Relations	Public Relations						
	Update Press Kit						
	Contact Editor						
	Press Release						
	Public Speaking						

CHAPTER FOURTEEN

Working With An Advertising Agency

As you have progressed through this book, you may have wondered how all these creative marketing materials would be produced. You're not a writer, designer or photographer by profession, which means that in many cases, especially in creating your Personal Brochure, Personal Postcard and Personal Logo, you'll be working with a creative or advertising agency.

Most ad agencies don't have Madison Avenue addresses. They're small shops that do work for local companies, and they will be more than happy to have your business. This chapter will explain to you how to work successfully with design or advertising agencies in creating your Personal Marketing materials.

One bit of advice: as you know, this book was written by Millennium Advertising, the creators of Personal Marketing for financial advisors. While we won't promote ourselves over another creative agency in your area, we would love to work with you on your Personal Marketing. Feel free to contact us with any of your questions at 888-730-5300. If you choose not to use Millennium Advertising for your Personal Marketing, be prepared to spend 10 to 15 hours educating your agency about the intricacies of your business.

Why Use an Ad Agency?

You've seen brochures and other materials created by financial advisors. How do they look and read? Let's just say they don't make the best impression. That's because advertising, writing and graphic design are intricate skills which take years to master. You don't have those skills, and in starting your Personal Marketing journey, you need to hire people who do.

Ask yourself this: would you hire a graphic designer to develop a retirement plan for you? Of course not. Hire professionals and you'll be astonished at the quality of the final product in look, feel and quality of storytelling.

Who to Hire

When it comes time to create your marketing materials, you have several choices:

- You can hire individual creative professionals who work independently, such as a solo writer and a solo designer.

- You can hire a design agency that will outsource your writing work.

- You can hire a full-service ad agency with all resources in-house.

Hiring a full-service agency will be the most expensive, but if you can afford it, that's what we recommend. Having a single point of contact for all your work, and a dedicated team working on all your materials, will not only help your work get finished more quickly, but help it be more consistent. More important, you should have one captain of the ship. You are in charge of your marketing, so hire someone to head up the creative work if you are not going to do it yourself.

Ad Agency Services You'll Need

If you decide to let the professionals do all the work in creating your Personal Marketing tools, these are the services you'll be paying for:

- Copywriting – Writing your materials, developing the concepts behind them; writing your slogan.

- Graphic design – Laying out your materials, choosing colors, photos and typefaces.

- Logo design – Creating your logo using your icon, name and slogan.

- Production – Assembling digital files for printing, producing the film or paper "plates" for your printer.

- Printing – Running your final printed pieces on a printing press, including stapling, binding, folding and cutting.

You may choose to handle your own printing, in which case you'll pay for production and be given the materials to give to your printer. Take our advice: let your agency handle the printing as well. It will cost a little more, but you'll have trained eyes looking at your materials to ensure quality.

You may also need the following optional services:

- Custom photography – Photo shoots with a professional photographer.

- Use of royalty stock photography – Paying for the right to use stock images from one of many companies.

- Illustration – Drawing, painting or computer generating original graphic images.

- Ad space buying (media buying) – Determining what magazine space, billboard space or radio airtime is best for your needs and target audience, negotiating price, and closing the deal.

What Does It Cost?

Costs of hiring creative professionals will vary, depending on the route you choose:

- Hiring independent writer and designer – You'll probably pay them hourly for all work. Reasonable hourly rates for experienced professionals are $60-$90 per hour, depending on what part of the country you're in.

- Hiring a design team – You'll pay more if you go to a design firm as opposed to an individual. They will also mark up the cost of contracting your writing work to a freelancer. Expect to pay $75-$90 per hour.

- Hiring an ad agency – There are many ways to pay an agency: monthly retainer, hourly, or a flat rate for the entire project. Usually, you'll pay part of the total fee up front, with the rest due when the work is done. Rates are usually negotiable, but you should expect to pay from $95-$150 per hour when working with an agency.

These fees may seem expensive, but rest assured: YOU WILL GET WHAT YOU PAY FOR. If you hire a college student to create your materials for $15 per hour, they will look every bit as cheap.

Overall, creating your initial Personal Marketing materials – brochure, postcard and logo – shouldn't cost more than $5,000. That figure does not include printing, since costs will vary depending on how many pieces you have printed. Be careful and don't pay too much, but don't pay too little. You do get what you pay for.

The People You'll Work With

In working with a creative agency you will encounter a variety of people with unique jobs and responsibilities. Here's a brief primer on what they do and what you can expect from them:

- Creative Director – This is the person responsible for all creative work put out by the agency. They will probably not work directly on your account, but will supervise the creative team assigned to you, and will select the best writer and designer to work on your materials. The Creative Director will also oversee the quality of your work.

- Art Director – Responsible for all the design work in the agency. The Art Director is both an experienced designer and a team leader with conceptual ability and art knowledge. The Art Director may not work on your materials, but will definitely supervise and approve the quality of all work by your designer.

- Account Executive – Your point of contact with the agency. Your Account Executive is part relationship builder and part strategist, helping you choose the best tools for your needs, then keeping the flow of communication going between you and your creative team. This is your main contact.

- Copywriter – The writer who develops the concepts behind your Personal Marketing pieces, writes the text, headlines and slogan, and determines how to best communicate with your audience. Your writer will generally work closely with your designer.

- Designer – The person who lays out your copy, photos, graphics and other elements into a desktop publishing program, creating the digital file that will become your Personal Brochure or Postcard. Designers will choose type, crop photos, create illustrations, and choose colors for your pieces.

- Production Manager – The person who handles the transition of your materials from computer files to print-ready pieces. Your Production Manager will keep your project on schedule, ensure that projects are typeset properly, and that you receive and approve proofs for all materials before they go to print.

The Process

So you've chosen to work with an ad agency. What happens next? We've provided you with a step-by-step outline of the likely things that will occur once you decide to hire a creative team. Of course, these can vary depending on who you use, but the flow is basically the same in any environment.

- The Creative Interview – After you've agreed on price and signed a contract, you'll meet with the Creative Director or Art Director, your Account Executive, and either a Writer, Designer, or both. The purpose: to talk about you, your goals, your business, and get an idea of what you want to say to your customers. If you've absorbed the Personal Marketing information found in this book, try compiling a "dossier" on yourself that talks about your Personal Marketing goals, your storytelling direction, your position, and your target audience. Aside from helping your agency tremendously, it will win you big respect points.

- The Creative Brief – Most ad shops will follow up your initial interview with a Creative Brief – a document which lays out the details of what you discussed, your goals and objectives, and the writing, design and strategic direction the agency thinks will work best for you. It's a blueprint for your marketing campaign, and your first chance to give feedback.

- Once you've approved the Creative Brief, you'll move onto a first draft. Generally, copy will be submitted to you before design, since the concepts and ideas of your writer will affect the design of your piece. Usually, you'll receive a text file to read and review, then the text will be laid out in your design and you'll be given a color copy of your piece to review as well.

- Revisions – You'll need to read your text and look over your design and be critical. Your agency needs you to provide feedback about things you don't like. You'll have at least one revision meeting by phone or in person to go over anything you don't like about the writing or the look of the pieces. Stick to your guns about things that displease you. One important note: agencies will generally ask you to "sign off" on a piece after revisions, stating that you have no more changes to make to that piece. If you sign off and then later discover something you want to change, you'll pay extra for the privilege.

- Final Draft – When all changes are made to copy and design, you'll be given final drafts of everything for review and approval. REVIEW THEM CAREFULLY. Even if you've read them 20 times already, read each word again. Find a colleague to review them, not for rewriting but for errors – typos, incorrect facts, etc. Once you give your written approval on this draft, your materials will go to print. No reputable agency will proceed with printing without your written approval on final drafts.

The Time is Up to You

How much time does all this work take? That is usually in your hands. If you ask 100 ad agencies what the biggest factor is in a project being done quickly, 99 will say "The responsiveness of the client." Ad agencies want to finish your job in a timely fashion so they can get paid, and you want to get the work done so you can have your materials. So you're working together. Here are some tips for helping get your Personal Marketing materials done as quickly as possible:

- Provide a file of information, especially about the Personal Marketing philosophy, to your agency. Unless you work with Millennium Advertising, your agency won't be familiar with Personal Marketing. Give them this book to read to familiarize them with Personal Marketing principles. Educate them up front about your position, your story, and the fact that you're not going the typical corporate marketing route.

- Get a set schedule from your agency on when deliverables are due – copy first draft, design first draft, and so on. Hold them to it.

- Be responsive about revisions! We can't emphasize this enough. If your brochure proof sits on your desk for three weeks, you're wasting everyone's time. Get revisions back to your agency in 48 hours. Agencies love clients who are efficient and respond quickly.

- Pay your agency on time. Some shops will start work before payment is received, as long as they trust you. Others will wait until a check is in their hands. Don't risk delays. Pay any advance fees immediately. Your agency will figure that if you're professional enough to pay them right away, they owe you the same kind of professional treatment.

- Communicate. Return calls and e-mails as soon as possible. The faster questions are answered, the faster the work will get done.

Making Your Ad Agency Experience Worthwhile

You're spending money for something that's utterly foreign to you. It's a little frightening. But consider what your investment in an advertising agency can do, besides giving you stellar Personal Marketing materials that will be the envy of all your colleagues. Ideally, you'll have a relationship with a long-term partner that can assist you with creating ads, new direct mail pieces, a Web site, PR for public events, and much more. A multi-skilled agency can be your best ally in growing your business.

Some general tips for making the most of your ad agency experience and investment:

- When searching for an agency, review their portfolio. Also, talk to some past clients and ask them to rate their experience.

- Talk to some small clients and see if the agency treats small fish as well as the big ones.

- Once you've chosen your agency, BE CANDID. This is the most important thing you can do in fostering a good relationship and getting the best work. Be open and direct about the work and the service you're receiving. If you don't like something, say so. If you have an idea you think will work better, bring it up. Candid, honest feedback is the best thing you can give your agency.

• If you don't like something, have a reason. Nothing will discourage creative people more than an "I don't like it but I don't know why" statement. Agencies hate clients who live by an "I don't know what I want, but I know what I don't like" philosophy. Don't be one of those clients.

• Trust your team. Sometimes, you may not understand why your writer wrote copy a certain way or chose a certain headline, or why your designer chose a certain photo for your brochure cover. In most cases, you should zip your lip and let them do their jobs. Remember, your materials need to be compelling to your clients, not necessarily to you.

• Be positive.

• Respect the creative process. Truly great creative work evolves from revisions and candid communication. Trust your team to use their creative judgment, tempered by your input.

Things to Know, Mistakes to Avoid

We're almost at the end of the first stage of your Personal Marketing journey. With luck, you've come to understand how Personal Marketing can not only help you grow your financial services business, but that it's critical to your very survival. In this final chapter, what we're giving you is very simple: like a wise old uncle, we're going to offer some good advice and some things to stay away from. As always, the aim is to make your Personal Marketing as successful as possible, and to help you make more money than ever.

Things to Know

1. People will copy you. It's as human as breathing: People see something that works and they steal it. It will happen with your Personal Marketing, assuming it's effective. Other financial advisors will copy your Personal Brochure, start putting out their own postcards and such. It's inevitable.

   Don't worry about the copycats. You have a powerful advantage: you were there first. Advisors who copy what you're doing, especially if they're foolish enough to go after the same target audience, will only look silly. In the meantime, when you see materials from a competitor that are obvious knock-offs of yours, don't panic. Use it as an opportunity to break out with some new marketing – a magazine ad, a new direct mail campaign, or perhaps a radio commercial.

Also, Nike does many TV commercials but does that stop competitors such as Reebok, Adidas or Converse from running their own costly campaigns? Of course not. They are constantly trying to out-do one another, or chase different markets. The same goes for you and your competition. If a competitor enters your market using Personal Marketing, protect your market share by looking for his weaknesses and exploiting them with Personal Marketing tactics.

2. Colleagues will scoff. If you work with a broker-dealer where you will come into contact with other advisors regularly, you'll get some sneers when you tell them how much money you've spent to create your Personal Marketing campaign. Don't let the doubts of the unenlightened take you off course. They haven't been educated about Personal Marketing, so as far as they're concerned the idea of you selling yourself, rather than no-load funds, is absurd. Let them go on thinking that. It makes them easier targets.

3. Good printing is worth every penny. We've touched on this subject lightly, but it bears repeating: don't go for rock-bottom-priced printing. The heft and feel of your Personal Marketing materials will tell prospects as much about you as the writing or design. You only get that glossy

shine, that thick paper, and that vivid color from a quality printer running your materials on a four-color press. When shopping for a printer, get a range of quotes and take the middle one, assuming that the printer's samples are of good quality. Cheap printing will give you cheap results.

4. You need to work with compliance. You may not like the idea of having your materials reviewed for NASD compliance, but you must. It's not just to protect your clients, but to protect you from liability for misleading claims. Simply be sure to run your marketing materials past your broker-dealer's compliance department before going to print.

5. Update your materials regularly. At the outside, have your materials redone every three years. Just like a musician or actor who renews his image every couple of years, you should do the same. Update your brochure's content, and get current photos. A redo of a current brochure is not nearly as expensive as a new brochure.

6. Limit yourself to one target audience to start. No matter how large your staff or your budget, you should market to no more than one target audience when you first begin doing Personal Marketing. Why? Because you've got to provide personal attention to all those people, and you can't afford to be pushed beyond your limits. Stick with one audience for your first six months.

After that period, if you feel up to it, you can expand your marketing to your second and even third audience. And if you conduct your Personal Marketing campaign as we've directed, three audiences will bury you in new business.

7. Public causes create visibility. As your Personal Marketing program begins to run smoothly, look into getting involved in community events or causes. You can sponsor a golf tournament, give money to a shelter, or design a fundraising program for a local church. Getting involved directly in the community enhances your positive personal brand – and makes you feel good.

8. Keep your sales skills sharp. Remember, Personal Marketing isn't a closing tool. It's about getting hot prospects in your door with the mindset to listen to you. Once they're in, it's up to you to close them and make them clients. So while you're becoming a marketer, don't let your sales skills slip. Practice your in-person pitch and make sure it's as polished and appealing as your Personal Marketing materials.

9. Think about premiums and offers. Once you get heavily into direct mail, you'll need a grab bag of special offers and giveaways to attract people to call you or come in for an appointment. Be thinking about putting such premiums together. They can include: Special Reports about things like retirement savings or emerging markets, free portfolio analysis, savings on planning fees for a set period, free sub scriptions to financial publications, free financial software, gift certificates to local restaurants or hotels, free admission to your seminar which normally requires a ticket purchase, and so on.

10. Track your return on investment (ROI). Ultimately, Personal Marketing is about results. Tracking your return on investment is the only way to determine if what you're doing is working. By tracking the results from your direct

mail, channel marketing and referral generation efforts, you can see how much of your new business can be directly traced to Personal Marketing. Once you know that number, look at your overall income increase and see if the rise in marketing-related business has offset your costs. If so, then you have a positive ROI, and you're doing great! If not, don't worry. As with start-up companies, the cost of growth sometimes means waiting a few years to see a profit. But you won't wait that long if you maintain your Personal Marketing efforts.

11. Hire a Marketing Assistant. You either have an assistant or you are one. You and your assistant should lay out your year's marketing and he or she should implement it on a daily basis.

Mistakes to Avoid

1. Showing your materials to all your colleagues before they're printed. Don't do it. They'll all find fault with your brochure or postcard, and many will insist that you "need more about products" in your pieces. Spare yourself the pain of ignoring these comments and keep your materials to yourself.

2. Selling too many services in your materials. At some point in your Personal Brochure and other materials you're going to talk about the products and services you provide. When you do, don't tout yourself as the expert in stocks, mutual funds, tax reduction, insurance, estate planning, employee benefits, annuities and government bonds. You'll confuse everyone. Stick to a few strong areas of your business and position yourself accordingly. Being the area's premier

employee benefits expert will get you plenty of lucrative business.

3. Handing out tacky items with your new logo on them. You want to spread your brand identity, but giving out coffee mugs and memo pads with your Personal Logo stamped on them is second-rate marketing. If you want to create logo premiums, go for a classier look. Create tiepins, pens, money clips, and so on. Your Personal Marketing is a step up from the ordinary; make your promotional items the same way.

4. Not having e-mail. It's the fastest-growing form of communication on earth, yet it shocks us how many advisors don't have e-mail or simply don't check it. Get it, check it regularly, and use it to send a quick note to your clients periodically. You'll be amazed at the convenience.

5. Copying someone else's marketing. It's all right to use another advisor's marketing for inspiration, but outright copying makes you look lazy and like someone who wasn't smart enough to get there first. Be original; tap the resources of your ad agency for ideas and take a fresh approach. One proviso: ads and other marketing from non-financial sources are fair game for copying. But always steal from the best.

6. Having an out of date Web site. Web technology changes constantly, and new features and business development tools appear monthly. Have a savvy Web developer or programmer on your speed dial so you can get the latest news on the latest tools, and possibly integrate them into your site. It's also not a bad idea to take one of the many

seminars being held around the country on making the Web work for small business.

7. Not thinking like a business. Getting in the mindset of an entrepreneur is part of Personal Marketing. You must start operating like a small business, rather than a one-man show. Forge strategic alliances with banks or accounting firms to gain referral business. Track your competitors' activities and gauge how much market share they have. Computerize all your bookkeeping, ROI tracking and customer information. Make your business as efficient as possible and you'll be stunned how much money you'll save...and make.

8. Not using this book as a constant reference. Refer back to The Brand Called You regularly, whenever you need clarification of a term or just a reminder of why Personal Marketing works. It's your best resource.

A Final Word...

That's it. We don't have a diploma for you, but you've graduated from your first course in Personal Marketing. You've got the knowledge and insight now to take your financial practice to a new level of profitability, to dominate your market, and make more money in less time than you ever imagined. The rest is up to you.

If there is one piece of advice we could leave with you it is this: become a marketer. Read marketing books, attend marketing seminars, listen to marketing tapes and network with colleagues. Most importantly, spend time every day working on your marketing. Every day!

We'd love to hear from you if you have questions about Personal Marketing, or if you're interested in using Millennium Advertising as your ad agency. That is, after all, what we do. Either way, we wish you luck and wealth. But honestly, if you follow the Personal Marketing plans in this book and stick to them, luck is the last thing you'll ever need.

A Few Last Words...

1. Share this Book

   We wrote "The Brand Called You" to change an industry. You can help. If you've gotten as much out of this book as we put into it, pass it along to a colleague and help spread the word about Personal Marketing.

2. Get the Information Firsthand at a Seminar

   There's difference between reading about riding a bike and riding a bike. You can experience Millennium Advertising's Personal Marketing firsthand by attending one of our "The Brand Called You" seminars. We perform over 60 public seminars for financial advisors each year in almost every major city across the US. There are two ways:

   1) Go to our Web site at www.thebrandcalledyou.com and go to the seminar section to enroll.

   2) Ask your broker-dealer, RIA, insurance company or association to invite us out to speak. We speak at over 40 conferences per year and meeting coordinators listen closely to their constituents. Tell them about us. Give them our book and press them to have us speak.